College Sense:
What College and High
School Advisors Don't Tell
You about College

College Sense:
What College and High School Advisors Don't Tell You about College

Tawan Perry

iUniverse, Inc.
New York Lincoln Shanghai

College Sense: What College and High School Advisors Don't Tell You about College

iUniverse books may be ordered through booksellers or by contacting:

iUniverse
2021 Pine Lake Road, Suite 100
Lincoln, NE 68512
www.iuniverse.com
1-800-Authors (1-800-288-4677)

Because of the dynamic nature of the Internet, any Web addresses or links contained in this book may have changed since publication and may no longer be valid.

The views expressed in this work are solely those of the author and do not necessarily reflect the views of the publisher, and the publisher hereby disclaims any responsibility for them.

ISBN: 978-0-595-47509-4 (pbk)
ISBN: 978-0-595-71238-0 (cloth)
ISBN: 978-0-595-91780-8 (ebk)

Printed in the United States of America

This book is dedicated in memory of Femi Alabi, a mentor, teacher, friend, and brother. Thanks for supporting, trusting, and believing in me.

Contents

ACKNOWLEDGEMENTS

My journey through college and the ability to complete this book would not have been possible without the help of some very special people:

Family: Mama, Dad, my Grandmothers, Denise, Yolanda, Regina, Rick, Bruce, uncles, aunts, cousins, nieces and nephews

Friends: Tina—the one constant in my life, Justin, Leonora, Christopher T., Carlos, Melvin, Demetrius, Celeste, Harry, Chevon, Drew, and Rorie

Prince George's Community College: Janice, Beth, and Mary

Morgan State University: Dr. Wright, Mr. Gwynn, Dr. Brunson, Ruby, Ms. G, Christina J. and Mr. Perry

UMASS: Dr. Shederick McClendon, Dr. Bonita Barnes, Derrick, Jamal, Shekhar, April, Rachel, Michelle, Chris, Emi, and Mentha

I would also like to take the time to thank everyone else who has contributed to my success over the years. No matter how big or small. You know who you are.

Special thanks to Dr. Shederick McClendon and James Washington.

INTRODUCTION

Today's college students do not fit into one category. They come from different walks of life and vary in age, ability, socioeconomic status, experience, particular needs, ethnicity, and life stages. Some have other responsibilities outside of school, such as working full-time, raising a family, or both. This aspect of higher education makes it more diversified and more enriching for everyone involved. For many students, experiencing higher education is a means to an end, while for others, it is an end in itself.

Through my collegiate experiences, I have developed a vested interest in college students and an incredible appreciation for the transformative power of education. As a graduate of three distinctly different institutions and a professional at two others, I believe when students are given guidance and become beneficiaries of a post-secondary education, they become contributing members of their community and the world. Education is the great equalizer in a world full of inequalities. Thus, the educated create choices for themselves, while the uneducated are given choices. The more choices you have, the more possibilities. With education, individuals cannot only empower themselves, but they can also inspire and empower others. As a direct result of this enlightenment, I believe that when people are educated, they have the opportunity to move forward in learning and in life. Education is the main ingredient in solving many of society's challenges: ignorance, fear, mediocrity, hatred, and poverty.

In this book, I will give you advice about college that I learned as I proceeded through my educational experience. Please use this advice as a compass to find your own success in college. The college experience is not purely academic or social; rather, it is a combination of both. Completing college is not all about academic ability; it's about persistence and the proper utilization of resources.

I am not a superstar athlete, famed actor, or entertainer; I am just someone who pursued what I believed to be my path to success. We live in a society that perpetuates inequalities: however, we also live in a country where you can reach your goal, whatever it may be if you put forth the time and effort. Some people will say that we have a long way to go to reach equality for everyone. While that is certainly true, we cannot deny how far we have come. Education has been a major contributor to these achievements.

Life is too short not to reach for your goal. With an education, we all can turn our dreams into reality. Education promotes success in many ways because it increases your opportunities, improves your quality of life, and gives you the tools to improve your earning potential. Education is what you decide to make of it. If you embrace the transformative process that takes hold of you, education will take you to heights you could have never imagined.

OPERATING MANUAL: HOW IS THIS GOING TO WORK?

The advice that I plan to deliver to you will not be conventional. While many books focus on one aspect of college, such as the admissions process, finding scholarships, or the first year of college, my intent is to give advice from a holistic perspective. The college experience is both an academic and social experience. Whether it is maintaining a relationship, learning to live with a roommate, or working full-time to pay for college, your experiences outside of the classroom will have an impact on your academic performance. Likewise, your academic experience will have an affect on your social interactions. This book would not be complete if I did not attempt to cover a variety of topics related to student development. I have divided this section of the book into four chapters that address the topics that influence your success in college.

I understand that many things that students learn in college are through trial and error. However, I hope that this book will at least serve as a blueprint to help you begin to make meaning of your college experience. At the start of each chapter, you will find a list of questions that will be covered in the chapter. If you choose to do so, you can go directly to the section of your interest and find the topic you want to read. However, I hope that you will take the time to read every page, as all of the information will be relevant to your success. I hope that I have thought of everything to make your journey through college more successful.

High school students, current undergraduate college students—especially first year students, community college students, and transfer students can benefit from this advice. Use this book as a blueprint for college success, from finding a college to learning how to negotiate your college environment. An aspect of learning to navigate the college environment is learning the language; if you know the language, you have a better chance of understanding and preparing for the complexities of college. Therefore, this book is designed to provide advice about many phases and aspects of college.

A QUICK WORD ABOUT—Weaved throughout the entire book, this feature gives you additional information about a particular topic that may add to your success.

APPENDIX A, B, and C—At the very end of the book, you will find appendixes. In appendix A, I would like to share with you my personal journey that started with uncertainty and ended with success. My journey was unpredictable and at times, overwhelming. Like many students, I experienced peaks and valleys while in college. I hope you find this part of the book inspiring. Appendix B contains website resources for topics such as scholarships, college search information and institution accreditation. Appendix C contains recommended readings regarding scholarships, college success, and other useful reference books.

GLOSSARY—Throughout each section, key terms will be highlighted. When you see a highlighted word that you do not understand, go to the glossary in the back of the book for the definition.

Chapter One

Is College Right For Me?

"Education makes a people easy to lead, but difficult to drive; easy to govern, but impossible to enslave."

—*Omar N. Bradley*

"Obstacles are what people see when they take their eyes off the goal."

—*Unknown*

QUESTIONS COVERED IN THIS CHAPTER:

1. What is higher education and what are my choices?
2. Now that I know of some choices, what questions should I ask?
3. What are some things I should know when applying for college?
4. I am already in college, but I want to transfer. Can you tell me about the transfer process?
5. Is there anything else I need to know?

CREATE A VISION

Before you read this section, it is important that you learn the art of visualization. Although you may not realize it, visualization is a skill that you utilize everyday. Visualization is the method used to start the process in order to accomplish your goals. Simply, it is using your imagination positively to change your reality. Try to visualize what you are about to do and think of a goal or end result. Write it down and work towards it until it is accomplished. Everything you do in college has to do with vision. For instance, if you cannot see yourself earning an A on an exam, then you greatly minimize your chances. However, if you can visualize an A, you will do everything in your power to make it happen. Therefore, develop both long and short term visions and work toward achieving them.

Although the college experience is complex, attending and eventually graduating from college is not about being the smartest student. It is about persevering. Many students, although academically gifted, fail to graduate from college each year because they are unable to focus on their goals. Some of the most inspiring and resilient people that I have met in college are students with disabilities. I admire them because they do not make excuses, and they do not let their disabilities get in the way. They just get it done. Everyone has baggage when they come to school. Some students have families to sustain, bills to pay, or learning disabilities. Others may be first generation college students. Nevertheless, the fact remains that we all have challenges. We just have to commit to our goals. My friend Leonora's favorite saying is "people do what they want to do." This statement could not be closer to the truth. We live in a country where it was once forbidden to learn how to read and write if you were a slave. Yet, in spite of the danger, some managed to learn how to read and write. A former slave, Frederick Douglas, went on to become one of the foremost leaders of the abolitionist movement. Today, thousands of individuals and groups have defied the odds and accomplished great things. Like these people, you have the same ability to overcome insurmountable circumstances.

WHAT IS HIGHER EDUCATION AND WHAT ARE MY CHOICES?

Higher education is education provided by colleges, universities, vocational institutions, and professional schools where you can earn awards, academic degrees, diplomas, or certificates. Concisely, it is any institution that you attend beyond high school. These institutions are called **postsecondary institutions** and there are over 4,000 in the United States. Out of this huge number, you need to choose an institution that works for you. This is one of the most important messages contained in this book. If you do not choose the right institution, you could find yourself transferring early or even dropping out. On the other hand, if you choose an institution that fits you well, you will flourish academically and socially. Therefore, figure out what you value and if the institution can meet your needs. Even if you do not get your first choice, you have many other choices. Just make sure you give yourself enough time to explore these options.

A QUICK WORD ABOUT ... COLLEGES AND UNIVERSITIES

There is a difference between a college and a university. They are the most common terms that refer to institutions of postsecondary education. The first type of school is a college, an educational institution for **undergraduate** students. Colleges often have fewer students than universities and smaller class sizes. They are less research focused and more student-centered. The second type of school is a university, which is an institution that offers both undergraduate and graduate courses. In addition, a university offers degree programs in a wide range of areas of study, sometimes including professional programs, such as law, dental, or medical schools.

NOTE: For the purpose of simplicity, the word institution will be synonymous with the words college and university.

Types of Institutions

What kind of institution do you see yourself attending? Different types of institutions fit different kinds of people. The following descriptions will give you a better understanding of the different types of institutions:

Liberal Arts Colleges

Liberal arts colleges offer a broad base of courses in the humanities, social sciences, and sciences as compared to emphasizing professional training or a targeted course of study. For example, if you attend a liberal arts college, some of the courses and majors that might be offered are history, philosophy, literature, mathematics, biology, psychology, and English. Liberal arts colleges emphasize faculty teaching. Therefore, they have smaller class sizes and enrollments. Examples of liberal arts colleges include New College of Florida, St. Mary's College of Maryland, and Hampshire College. Liberal arts colleges are both private and public.

Private Universities and Colleges

Private universities and colleges rely on **tuition, fees,** endowments, and other private sources. Because private institutions do not rely on funding from the government, they usually have more say in how they govern their school. Private colleges and universities are usually smaller and can offer more personalized attention. However, private institutions are usually more expensive than public institutions. Examples of private colleges and universities include Smith College, University of Southern California, University of Dayton and Oberlin College.

Public Universities and Colleges

A public university usually offers more **majors** and research facilities. Class sizes may be bigger, and **teaching assistants** may teach classes rather than **professors**. Public universities are usually less expensive, particularly for in-state residents. They receive most of their money from the state or local government. Examples of public colleges include the Ohio State University, University of North Carolina, and Kent State University.

Community Colleges

These colleges attract and accept students from the local community. Community colleges usually offer two-year **associate's degrees**. Upon earning an associate's degree, you can enter a four-year institution with junior standing and then earn a bachelor's degree. Some community college programs do not award an associate's degree, but you can still enter a four-year school as a junior. Additionally, they offer continuing education courses that are instructional courses designed for **traditional** and **non-traditional students**. Community colleges offer technical programs that prepare students for immediate employment. Other names synonymous with community colleges are technical colleges, county colleges, junior colleges and city colleges. Examples of community colleges are Howard County Community College, Miami Dade College, and Sinclair Community College.

Online Institutions

Online Institutions are institutions that use the Internet and other instructional instruments to deliver education to students that are unable to be present in class. Although many institutions are beginning to offer online classes, these institutions offer classes that are online only. These institutions are ideal for working adults and students that live far away from an institution. Examples of online institutions include The University of Phoenix, Westwood College, and DeVry Technical Institute.

Ivy League

These institutions are some of the most prestigious and selective schools in the United States. With the exception of Cornell University, Ivy League institutions are privately owned and controlled. The Ivies are all located in the Northeast region of the United States. The Ivy League institutions are Princeton, Columbia, Harvard, Yale, Dartmouth, University of Pennsylvania, Brown, and Cornell.

Specialized, Career, and Technical Colleges

Specialized colleges emphasize preparation for specific careers such as art, business, seminary, and rabbinical. Vocational institutions (i.e., trade schools) usually train students in a specific career field, such as accounting, welding, cosmetology, automotive repair, computer technology, or the culinary arts. The entire course of study is often two years or less. Graduates earn a diploma, certificate, or an associate's degree.

Gender Specific Institutions (Women's Colleges and Men's Colleges)

Gender specific institutions are colleges where the student population is not co-ed. Instead, these colleges are either all-male or all-female colleges. More often than not, these colleges are private and/or religiously affiliated. They are also usually liberal arts colleges. Examples include Wabash College, Mount Holyoke College, Deep Springs College, and Morehouse College.

Religiously Affiliated Colleges

These institutions are private colleges and universities that are affiliated with a religious faith. Some religiously affiliated colleges are Gardner-Webb University, Xavier University (OH), and Brandeis University.

Minority-Serving Institutions

Minority Serving Institutions are institutions that make up a category of educational establishments including Historically Black Colleges and Universities (HBCUs), Hispanic-Serving Institutions (HSIs) and Tribal Colleges and Universities (TCUs). Many minority institutions were founded to create equal opportunities for minority students. These schools offer students a unique opportunity to experience an educational community in which they are part of the majority.

Historically Black Colleges and Universities (HBCUs)

These institutions were established prior to 1964. The original intent was to educate Black Americans. HBCUs were founded with the intent to counter-balance the mainstream educational system of the United States, which failed to educate Black Americans successfully. Today, HBCUs offer all students an opportunity to get an education. Examples of HBCUs include Spelman College, Morgan State University and Howard University.

Hispanic-Serving Institutions (HSIs)

HSIs are institutions that serve a predominantly Hispanic student population or that were historically founded within the U.S. Hispanic community. They are colleges, universities, or systems where total Hispanic enrollment constitutes a minimum of 25% of the total enrollment (i.e., full-time, part-time, and graduate). Despite this requirement and unlike HBCUs or TCUs, most HSIs do not have university missions that address distinctive purposes and goals for Latinos. Examples of HSIs include California State at Fresno, Long Beach City College and Barry University.

Tribal Colleges and Universities (TCUs)

Colleges and universities established by Native Americans that provide college students, with a way to preserve and teach more about tribal culture and language. TCUs offer vocational certificate programs, two-year associate degrees, and some offer **bachelor's** or **master's** degree programs. Examples of tribal colleges include Tohono O'odham Community College, Leech Lake Tribal College, Sitting Bull College, and Chief Dull Knife College.

When it comes to selecting an institution, what matters most is that the institution fits your specific needs and makes you feel comfortable. While sometimes students do not get it right the first time and have to transfer, it helps to do your research the first time around. Institutions of higher education are businesses first and foremost. Do not get caught up in the hype of going to the most prestigious and expensive university. While prestige can be a factor, the name alone does not guarantee success or a job after graduation. You as the student make the degree and not the other way around. The degree may get you the opportunity, but the rest is up to you. Once you select the type of institution you wish to attend, seek information about each institution and begin to narrow your choices. Again, a good institutional fit for you is the most important aspect to consider in choosing a college or university to attend.

"Life is about chasing after the things you think are truly worth it, even if they don't happen. I'd rather have nothing but know I didn't settle for something I didn't want!"

—*Selma Hayek*

NOW THAT I KNOW OF SOME CHOICES, WHAT QUESTIONS SHOULD I ASK?

In this section, I will list some questions to consider before, during and after the campus visit. The best place to start looking for these answers is the **college catalogue** or Website. Once you visit the Website or catalogue, the next best thing is to arrange a campus visit. Most institutions provide campus tours free of charge. In order to arrange a campus visit, call the institution's admissions office. Another option is to go to a school's open house or welcome day. Open houses are designated dates when schools arrange a time for prospective students and parents to tour the campus. Most institution's open houses consist of a particular college (e.g., college of Arts and Science, School of Business, etc.) at the school giving information about their programs. For example, if you are interested in majoring in Electrical Engineering, the School of Engineering at the institution will have a day where you may be able to meet the **dean** of your school, current students, professors, and other **administrators**. In addition to asking the tour guide questions, you should ask current students about their experience. Students are usually very willing to answer questions and, unlike staff members or administrators of the institution, they will give you a response from a student perspective.

> "3rdAgreement: Don't Make Assumptions Find the courage to ask questions and to express what you really want. Communicate with others as clearly as you can to avoid misunderstandings, sadness, and drama. With just this one agreement, you can completely transform your life."
>
> —*Don Miguel Ruiz*

Questions to consider <u>before</u> the campus visit:

Admission Questions
What is the **admission** application fee?
Which credits will transfer?

Financial Questions
What is the price of tuition for my standing? (In-state residents, out-of-state residents, and international students?)
Is there an additional fee for taking more than 15 credits? (Some institutions charge a flat fee for an unlimited amount of credits, while other institutions do the opposite.)

General Questions

Is there a first year or transfer orientation program?

Is the institution on a quarter or semester system? (This may affect course and grade transfer.)

Do I want to go to a public or private institution?

Which do I prefer, a small school or a big school?

How close or far away do I want to be from my family?

Do I want an in-state school or an out-of-state school?

Does the school have my program/major?

What do I value the most? What do I value the least?

What type of academic experience am I looking to gain from this institution?

What type of social experience am I looking to gain from this institution?

What immunization shots are required?

Are summer classes typically offered?

Does the school accept **CLEP** credit or **advanced placement (AP)** classes from high school?

What entrance exams are required?

What happens if I do not test into college-level courses?

What if I am home-schooled? What will I need to apply?

Institutional Questions

Is the institution accredited? If so, what is the accrediting association?

Where does my major rank nationally?

What is the institution's mission statement?

When and why was the college established?

What makes this institution unique?

Resource Questions

What types of services are available for students with learning disabilities?

What types of services are available for students with physical disabilities?

Questions to consider <u>during</u> the campus visit:

Academic Related Questions

What is the student to faculty/instructor ratio?

Are the faculty members approachable?

Are the faculty members available?

What types of internships are commonly available for students in the department?

Admission Questions
Is there **rolling admissions**?
What is the retention rate for students? What is the retention rate for minorities? What is the retention rate of 1st and 2nd year students?

Financial Questions
How much aid or scholarship is available for incoming or transfer students? Are these **scholarships** renewable every year?
Can I use financial aid funds to pay for books and supplies?
What are the academic requirements for renewing the financial aid award?
Is the tuition projected to increase over the next year(s)?
What types of **work-study** jobs are available to students?
If awarded a full scholarship, will it include fees and/or books?
Are payment plans available? If so, when are payments usually due?
What are the terms and conditions in my aid package (e.g. treatment of outside scholarships, **loan** repayment policies, renewal criteria, etc.)?
Does the institution accept payment via credit card?
Is there an option to pay tuition, room and **board** monthly?
Are late fees assessed if the bill is not paid by the deadline?
How many times a year will I be billed?

General Questions
If I live in another state, how do I plan to get home for the holidays?
How far is the bus station/airport? What type of transportation services does this institution offer (shuttle buses, taxis)?
Is this largely a residential campus or commuter campus? (This may dramatically affect your social experience on the weekends.)
Are freshmen that live on campus allowed to park their vehicles on campus during their first year?
Is there adequate parking on campus?
Is there adequate shopping and/or public transportation near the school?
Does the institution offer its students health insurance coverage?
Where is the nearest hospital?
Do students typically go home on the weekends?
Are there any discounts offered by local vendors?

What is the average temperature for each season?
What type of weekend activities does the institution offer?

Institutional Questions

How many libraries and/or learning spaces does this institution have?
Am I required to purchase a laptop/notebook?
What is the crime rate of the institution? What is the crime rate of the neighboring city or town?
What holidays does the institution observe?
What types of breaks (Fall Break, Spring Break, etc.) are offered during the school year?
What is the breakdown of minority students?
What is the institution's alcohol policy?

Residence Hall/Housing Questions

What are some of the safety features in my **residence hall**?
Does the residence hall offer **living learning communities**?
Are the classrooms and residence halls equipped with central heating and cooling systems?
How many people typically live in a residence hall? What types of renovations have taken place recently?
How many laundry facilities are available in this residence hall?
What type of access is available to get inside the building?
Does this residence hall have security cameras?
Are the residence halls open during short breaks/holidays/winter break?
What is the procedure in the residence hall if you are leaving over winter break? Do you have to take your things with you?
Is there a curfew for students? What is the visitation policy?
What is the guest policy?
Are all of the residence halls Internet capable? If so, is the service wireless, Ethernet, or other?
Are there pest problems in the residence halls?
Is there a housing application waiver?
How much is the housing **security deposit**?
Am I required to get voicemail or on-campus phone service?
What are the options for meal plans? Must I purchase a meal plan?
Is there 24-hour coverage at the front desk?
How do I report maintenance issues?
How many semesters or years can a student reside in the residence hall?

What types of off-campus housing options—apartments, landlord-owned homes, etc.—are available to students?
Are you allowed to bring candles, hotplates, or other cooking appliances?
What is the residence hall's pet policy?
Is there upper-class student housing?

Resource Questions
How many libraries do you have, and what services do they provide?
What types of services are their available for those who are considered a minority?
Any services available that are designed especially for women/men?
How many student organizations are on campus? Where can I find them?
Is the **Alumni** Association active with undergraduate students?
What type of cultural centers do you have on campus?
What kind of **service learning projects** does the campus offer?
What type of spiritual services does the campus offer?
Is this campus LGBT friendly? What support services or organizations are available?
What types of services are available for students with disabilities?
What kind of religious centers are there on and off campus? If off campus, how far away from campus are they?
What kind of leadership programs are offered to students?
Does the campus have a study-abroad office?
What is the international student population? What services are available for them?
If applicable, what time does the gym or recreational facility close?
Is there a bank and/or ATM on campus?
What services are offered in the health center?
Is the counselor or nurse available 24 hours a day? How long does it usually take to get in to see a doctor for routine care?
Are childcare services available? Are there student discounts available?

Questions to consider <u>after</u> the campus visit:

Financial Questions
How much will my financial aid or other aid cover?
What will happen if my financial situation changes in another year?
When can I expect to receive bills from the institution?

General Questions
How much spending money will I need for other expenses?

What did I like the most about the institution? Why?

What did I like the least about the institution? Why?

Is this a party school?

Can I get a similar experience for a lower price somewhere else?

Is the campus accessible for handicapped students?

What was the campus environment like? Did people seem welcoming or friendly?

Can I see myself at this institution?

What types of things (toilettes, bedding, etc.) will I have to buy?

A QUICK WORD ABOUT ... CAMPUS QUESTIONS

If you are not comfortable with asking the campus guide some of the more difficult questions, you may want to contact specific offices prior to your campus tour to set up an individual visit. Alternatively, you may want to ask these questions over the telephone, through email or written correspondence. Campus departments have detailed information on their Websites and often, an email button where you can ask more questions or request detailed information.

While the research is time-consuming, remember that you are making one of the most important investments of your life. You are also making a long-term commitment. Please note that these questions are by no means comprehensive. Take the time to make your own list and ask the questions about things that you value.

WHAT ARE SOME THINGS I SHOULD KNOW WHEN APPLYING FOR COLLEGE?

"Education, then, beyond all other devices of human origin, is the great equalizer of the conditions of man, the balance wheel of the social machinery."

—*Horace Mann*

A QUICK WORD ABOUT ... ACCREDITATION

Be sure that your institution is accredited by a nationally recognized post-secondary accreditation institution. Accreditation is the process by which an educational institution's services and operations are voluntarily examined by an accrediting agency to determine if applicable standards are met. Your first task when selecting schools should be to verify accreditation. This information is highlighted on the institution's Website and in the catalogue. If your institution is not accredited, you will be wasting valuable time and money. Also, if an institution is not accredited, it is very likely that your courses will not transfer. Be especially aware that a school's acceptance of financial aid does not mean that they are accredited. You can check various Websites listed in Appendix B to discover which postsecondary institutions are accredited. In addition to institutional accreditation, be sure to check for departmental and program accreditation as well.

In this section, I will briefly cover the basics of the application and **admission** process for colleges and universities. While I will not go into great detail about the process involved, I will give you an idea about how the process works.

College and University Admission Process

If you plan to attend a four-year college or university, you will need to take either the **ACT** or **SAT** tests as part of their admissions process. Although every school has a range of differing application requirements, it is a safe bet that you will need to fill out an application and provide a copy of your high school academic **transcript**. Some schools also require an essay, **portfolio**, or interview.

Advantages to starting your postsecondary journey at a four-year institution are:

- Greater opportunities to interact socially with other students, especially if you live on campus
- More opportunity to live in a residence hall with peers in your age range
- Better access to campus resources
- Easier transfer of courses
- More class and scheduling opportunities

- Prestige
- An opportunity to learn how to be independent
- Less transportation costs if you live on campus

Considerations/Disadvantages to starting your postsecondary journey at a four-year institution are:

- Cost of attendance (always more expensive)
- Shrinking budgets may cause frequent tuition increases
- Sometimes a lack of varied diversity
- Less individualized attention from faculty (specifically, large public universities)
- Academic and social pressures
- Sometimes less assistance for a variety of learners (no remedial and/ or orientation classes)

Community College Admission Process

For starters, if you are planning to attend a community college, please be aware that most community colleges have an open admissions policy. This means that you do not need to take the SAT or ACT in order to be accepted by the college. This admissions policy does not mean that these colleges have lower standards than four-year institutions. Generally, you will need a high school diploma or GED to be admitted into a community college. For many students, this takes away a great deal of pressure from trying to obtain the required ACT or SAT score before graduating from high school.

However, many community and technical colleges require an assessment test that can be taken prior to orientation and registration in mathematics, reading and writing. Depending on your scores, you may be placed in developmental courses to improve your skills and test scores. However, do not think of this as a set back. Developmental courses will help you improve your skills to be a successful college-level student.

Moreover, once you have attended a community college for at least a semester and taken your **general education requirements**, you can transfer to another school of your choice. If you complete two years of community college and maintain a high GPA, there is a good chance that aid will be available upon transferal into a four-year institution. You will start out with junior status at the new institution (pending credit transferal and credits completed). Therefore, you will not have to repeat first year level classes (e.g., English 101, Biology 101, etc.). Also, your degree will be from the four-year institution even though the first two years were completed at a community college. If you are planning to transfer after one or two years at community college, speak with your advisor about transfer agreements. Often, community colleges have **articulation agreements** with four-year campuses which state the transfer courses that are accepted into their program. This information will be available in the counseling, advising or registration center.

Advantages to starting your postsecondary journey at a community college are:

- Less expensive (especially if you reside in the city or county of the college)
- Close to home
- Requires only a GED or high school diploma
- Helps improve deficiencies through developmental courses
- Typically provides more individualized attention from teachers
- More diversity among student population
- Provides more accessibility for students with disabilities
- Offers more assistance for a variety of learners
- Provides limited academic and degree programs but a variety of career and technical choices

Considerations/Disadvantages to starting your postsecondary journey at a community college are:

- Very limited student housing
- Credits are not always transferable
- Classes are smaller and may fill up faster
- Commuter costs (gas, food, etc.)
- In most cases, a 4-year degree is not offered
- Limited social life

"Life does not require us to be the biggest or the best, it asks only that we try."

—Unknown

In summary, when attending a four-year college or university, you pay for a social experience as well as an academic education. However, when attending a community college, you pay for just the academic education. Although community colleges have student activities and organizations, the likelihood of getting socially involved at the community college level is slim because most students do not stick around after classes. They usually go home or go to work. However, whatever type of institution you decide to attend, you must consider the type of experience you are looking for and what you value.

THE COLLEGE APPLICATION

One of the first things to remember when applying to college is to know when the admission application is due. For instance, if you want to attend college in September, you should submit everything no later than March. If you wish to attend the college during the spring semester, which usually begins in January at most institutions, you will need to submit your completed application no later than October. Check with the school with which you are interested for their exact deadline. You can do this by checking the school's website or calling the admissions office. In addition, the application process for applying to several schools can be time consuming. Find out if you can use a **Common Application** or another electronic application to cut down on the paper work.

No matter how you plan to apply, you will need most of the following information:

- Personal information (like your Social Security Number)
- Family information (like parents' names, addresses, and Social Security Numbers)
- Educational background (where you went to high school)
- Test scores (SAT and/or ACT)
- Academic experience (specific courses you have taken)
- Awards and honors
- Extracurricular activities (including school, religious, civic, work, sports, and volunteer)

- Written essay
- Recommendations from teachers and counselors
- An official high-school transcript

Source: www.adventuresineduction.com

APPLYING FOR FINANCIAL AID

Financial aid eligibility is based on the amount of income you report. If you, your parents, or guardian make over a certain amount, you may not be eligible. If you are eligible for financial aid, you should fill out your paperwork immediately. Due to deadlines, you can find yourself out of free money if you fail to fill out your paperwork immediately. You can do so by going online and filling out a **FAFSA** (Free Application for Federal Student Aid). For more information, go to www.fafsa.ed.gov.

If you are planning to start in the fall semester, the best time to fill out your application is January of the year you plan to enroll. Even if you do not have all of your paperwork, you should still send in your materials, so that the procedure can begin. Remember; the longer you wait to fill out paperwork, the longer it will take to process. In turn, the wait can affect the amount of aid you receive. In most cases, the institution awards more money because the money is still available. For every day that you wait to put in paperwork, another student is receiving money from the same source.

In addition, once you have completed a FAFSA, you will not have to complete the full form again the upcoming year. Rather, you should receive a renewal FAFSA via the web or mail. Because much of your information will not change, the Renewal FAFSA will include your responses from the previous year. Take time to review those responses to make sure they are still accurate, and answer any remaining questions.

Note: If your student status changes from full-time to part-time during the academic year, your financial aid award will be automatically adjusted.

Key Questions to Ask Before and After Applying for Financial Aid:

1. Am I using my information or my parent/guardian's information?
2. How much do my parent(s) or guardian(s) make?
3. Am I eligible to be classified as an independent student?

4. What is the maximum aid per year provided by the institution?

5. What kinds of other aid am I qualified to receive?

6. If I take out a loan, will I need a co-signer? What forms are required to complete the financial aid process, and what is the priority deadline for applying for financial aid?

7. When will I be notified about the financial aid decision?

8. On what basis are financial aid decisions made at a particular institution?

9. How much will the total cost of attending this institution increase each year?

I AM ALREADY IN COLLEGE, BUT I WANT TO TRANSFER. CAN YOU TELL ME ABOUT THE TRANSFER PROCESS?

"I have not failed 10,000 times. I have successfully found 10,000 ways that will not work."

—*Thomas Edison*

"Perseverance and tact are the two most important qualities for the individual who wants to move ahead."

—*Benjamin Disraeli*

Applying for college for the first time is complex enough, but the process of transferring can be just as problematical if you are not sufficiently prepared. If you are preparing to transfer, you will need to speak with a transfer advisor immediately. The transfer advisor should be one of the first persons you get to know on a campus if you are planning to transfer. They are important for several reasons. First, transfer advisors are up to date with what it takes to transfer successfully. Second, they will prevent you from taking classes that may not transfer. Third, the advisor may have information about various scholarships and aid that is offered at your next institution. Finally, they are usually familiar with the **articulation** process and other transfer policies.

In addition to speaking with a transfer advisor, you should take other steps before you transfer to another institution. First, prepare for your transfer early. If you plan to transfer after your first year, you will have to consider deadlines for admission and financial aid. Inquire if the institution's admission process is a **rolling admissions** or standard process. Whatever the case may be, the institution you wish to transfer into has early fall deadlines established for students planning to transfer in the spring.

Second, take time to research articulation agreements. In many instances, articulation agreements often have geographic restrictions. If you plan to attend an in-state institution, you may have difficulty transferring credits out-of-state without losing a great deal of credits. Again, speak with your transfer advisor/counselor to find out about the policies of the school to which you wish to transfer. Lastly, if an institution does not accept your credits, you may appeal the decision. In order to appeal, you will first need to gather information about their appeals procedure. Appeals (sometimes called petitions) are granted at the discretion of the admissions office. You can request this form from an admissions officer.

Factors that affect credit transferal:

- **Time limits:** Policies differ from school to school, but many schools have time limits on **transfer credits**. If the credits you hope to transfer were earned three years ago, check the credit transfer policies at the four-year school.

- **Accreditation:** If a school is not accredited, chances are the institution's courses will not be transferable.

- **College and/or state transfer policies:** Colleges determine which credits they will accept, with some schools influenced by statewide articulation programs.

- **Relevance of the course:** Institutions tend to accept credits from programs and courses that are similar to those they offer.

- **Course Grades:** Applicants must meet minimum grade requirements for their credits to transfer. For example, if you earned a D in a class, that may not be acceptable to the institution because they may require a minimum of a C.

Source: www.fastweb.com

Transferring Credits

Ultimately, to make the most of the transfer process, you need to be proactive. Be sure that the school to which you are transferring is on the same type of academic year. For example, if you attend an institution that has a semester system, do not transfer to a school that has a **quarter system**. If you do so, a good chance exists that your credits will not transfer. Although it may be the same class, the quarter and semester systems are very different. Plan early and do not hesitate if you need help.

IS THERE ANYTHING ELSE I NEED TO KNOW?

"Belief is the thermostat that regulates all success."

—Anonymous

As with anything else, making the transition to college or transferring from one college to another is both a complex and a long process with much to consider:

GETTING MONEY

You can finance your education several different ways: working full-time at the institution, scholarships, **grants**, payment plans, student loans, and work-study. With regard to scholarships, many universities have scholarships that are offered by many different departments. Some of the best places to start investigating if a college has scholarships are the institution's **Honors Program**, Alumni Office, **Schools** or **Colleges** at the institution, Financial Aid Office, College Foundation or Athletic department.

Just be sure that you do not limit yourself only to what the institution has to offer. Many organizations outside of the institution and individuals provide scholarships for students. Some other places you can look besides the university are churches, parishes, fraternities and sororities, service organizations, local politicians—such as the senator or delegate that represents your distinct, local businesses, corporate organizations (e.g., Burger King, Target, etc.), charity organizations, and non-profit organizations. Also, do not be afraid to ask relatives or friends of the family for money. You might just be surprised. Some time ago, I knew a student who asked a friend of the family for money for college. The person's employer sponsored a scholarship for students who were first-generation college students. To make a long story short, the student applied and was awarded $2,000! Therefore, it never hurts to ask, but it will hurt if you miss out.

A QUICK WORD ABOUT … PAYING FOR TUITION

When I first started college, I often wondered why students who were children of the employees at the college wanted to attend the school where they knew that they would see their parents every day. At the time, the best answer that I could think of was that the parent wanted to keep a watchful eye on their child. After asking questions, I soon discovered that it had nothing to do with my original thought. Rather, it had more to do with receiving a free education. If your parent(s) or guardian works at the institution, you might qualify for reduced or free tuition. At some institutions, part of the employee benefits package offered can be free tuition, reduced tuition, or tuition reimbursement for spouse and dependents. The only stipulation that usually matters is length of employment and full-time status. For that reason, if you are a student and you want to go to school for free, either get a full-time job at the school or see if your parents can work at the institution. Literally, it pays!

ROOMMATES OR FLOORMATES?

In considering leaving home or transferring from one institution to the next, you should definitely think about whether you want to live on-campus or off-campus.

If you plan to live on campus, expect the following pros and cons:

- A more structured environment (rules, more accountability)
- Easier access to campus resources (Internet, library, laundry facilities)
- Greater opportunities to get involved in campus organizations
- Instant community (social and extracurricular)
- Easier access to classes
- A greater opportunity to meet more people
- Limited privacy

- Limited Internet downloading and file sharing
- Adherence to guest, visitation, or curfew policy
- Sharing common places (study area, bathroom)
- Possible relocation when the university is closed

On the other hand, if you plan to live off campus, expect the following pros and cons:

- More privacy
- Less structured environment
- Campus Commute
- No guest, visitation, or curfew policy
- Limited opportunities to get involved
- Less access to classes
- Limited access to campus resources
- Private common places (bathroom, kitchen)
- No relocation in summer months (You may be able to sign a lease for the entire year.)

I CANNOT DECIDE. ARE THERE OTHER OPTIONS?

If you like the conveniences of living on campus but the benefits of living off campus, you should consider an on-campus apartment (if this option exists). On campus apartments or houses are usually not available to first-year students. You should contact the institution's Housing or Residence Life department for more information about alternate housing options.

A QUICK WORD ABOUT ... SECURING HOUSING

If you plan to live on campus, you should contact the institution's housing department as soon as possible to begin the process of securing a room for the upcoming school year. As soon as you are accepted, you should begin the process. The day of your initial visit, you should speak with someone in the housing office about reserving a space. At some institutions, housing assignment offices will allow you to reserve a space as long as you have been admitted to the university. If you reserve a spot and then decide to attend another institution later, the worst that could possibly happen is for you to lose your application fee. You can expect the application fee to be anywhere from $30 to $80. Also, if you already have a roommate in mind, be sure to inform the housing offices. If you notify the housing assignment office in advance, there is a good chance that your requests will be taken into consideration.

As previously stated, institutional fit is very important. However, along with institutional fit, realistic expectations are just as important. Several students want to attend the brand name school or the institution that is at the top of the *US News University and College Ranking Report*, but every year without fail, students depart institutions because the school fails to meet their expectations. However, it is not always the school's fault in this matter because as hard as some schools may try, they can never instill in a student the proper motivation for seeking out the services required to succeed. This is the student's responsibility and it is the institution's obligation to provide services. Just remember to be realistic in choosing your school. It is not about being enrolled in college; it is about having a good experience and ultimately graduating. Graduating from college requires a commitment by both the student and the institution.

IMMUNIZATION SHOTS

In order to enter college or transfer schools, you must get specific shots before you can be admitted to the institution. Although each institution's requirements vary, some of the most common immunizations that you will need are hepatitis A and/or B, meningococcal conjugate vaccine (MCV4), meningitis, tetanus, mumps, rubella, and flu. Even if your institution does not require you to get these shots, it is a good idea to get them anyway. Living in such close proximity is a breeding ground for germs, diseases, and bacteria. If you cannot afford some of the vaccinations, the health center usually has a listing of local places you may be able to get vaccinations free of charge. Be sure to check out your school's immunization requirements before you move into campus housing.

A quick review of the college admissions process:

1. Decide the type of institution you want to attend
2. Begin the college research process (go to college fairs, research websites)
3. Take the SAT or ACT (if required)
4. Secure official academic transcripts
5. If eligible, apply for financial aid and other scholarships
6. Select schools to visit (attend open houses)
7. Determine college selections
8. Fill out admission form/application (apply to more than one school)
9. Wait for the acceptance letter
10. Decide on housing options
11. Secure housing (submit application, **security deposit**)
12. Get required immunization shots

Chapter Two

I've Made It! Now What Should I Do?

"Nothing takes the place of persistence."

—Calvin Coolidge

"A journey of a thousand miles must begin with a single step."

—Laotzu

QUESTIONS COVERED IN THIS CHAPTER:

1. What should I do first before I arrive on campus?
2. Who are some of the people that I should get to know?
3. I am still lost. Could you give me an action plan?
4. I think I got it. What other advice should I know?

WHAT SHOULD I DO FIRST BEFORE I ARRIVE ON CAMPUS?

Take time to explore your college catalogue, website, and student handbook. These resources can help you better understand course offerings, completion requirements, and where to locate campus resources. You can avoid many mistakes if you take the time to read the campus catalogue. Students usually under utilize this book. I have known students to miss many opportunities because they failed to read the campus catalogue. Even worse, I have known students who did not graduate on time because they failed to take a required class that was clearly listed in the catalogue. While I know that reading the catalogue may not be on your personal "to read" list, it does save you time and money. Also, do not forget that the year in which you entered your respective institution is the year of the catalogue that you must follow. Therefore, if the catalogue changes from your first year to your senior year (as it probably will), you will only be held accountable for the requirements and **prerequisites** of the catalogue year you enrolled at the institution.

WHO ARE SOME OF THE PEOPLE THAT I SHOULD GET TO KNOW?

When students think of university resources, they usually think about people who work in the offices. While that certainly makes sense, one of the most overlooked resources in college is your peer group. A wealth of experience and expertise exists at your fingertips both in the classroom and on campus. When I was a **Resident Assistant (RA)**, I could ask anyone on my floor for help. I knew peers who could help me with math, science, and history. In addition, I found peers who could cut my hair, help me prepare for interviews, and assist me with computer problems. As one of my **mentors** told me, "at an institution of higher learning, you should never be afraid to ask for help." So, be open to assistance even if it just kills you to ask for help.

If you plan to live on-campus, you should get to know these individuals:

Resident Assistants—(also referred to as Resident Advisor, Community Assistants, etc.) This seasoned student leader lives on your floor in the residence hall and is there to assist you. They usually know things about the school and if they do not, they can point you in the right direction. At most institutions, they are your most important resource. They are usually among the first people you meet.

Residence Directors—(also referred to as Community Director, Hall Director, Area Coordinator, etc.) Similar to high school principals, they manage all of the operations of the residence halls. Residence Directors are live-in educators who are professionally trained to mediate and resolve crises. Additionally, they supervise the RAs. They are some of the most informed and knowledgeable professionals at the institution because they often collaborate with other offices and departments on campus.

Professors—Because professors issue your grades, their opinion matters considerably. Although some professors may seem unobtainable because they have limited office hours (specific hours that professors set aside to meet with students), it would be wise to attempt to meet with them outside of class at least once during the semester. If the professor or teaching assistant can place a name with a face, that can make the difference in a grade (especially if the grade is borderline). Visiting professors during office hours can also help clear up confusion about upcoming tests, assignments, and the course **syllabus.**

Administrative Assistants—Get to know the administrative assistants of different offices. They are perhaps the most important people in the office because they are the gatekeepers of the person with whom you wish to make contact. They decide when you are able to see the people with whom you need to speak. Either you can be a familiar face or you can be just another student that comes to the office. It pays to get to know them personally because they are usually knowledgeable about information that others in the office will not know.

Tutors—I cannot say enough about the students who can lead you to the promised land, graduation. Tutors are helpful in two ways: First, they assist with understanding course assignments, quiz and test review. Second, being high achievers themselves, they can help you find scholarships and other financial aid. At many institutions, tutors are honor students who are in good graces with the offices that award the scholarships. They can also provide advice on courses to take.

Special Interest/Multicultural/Office Staff Members—If you are from an underrepresented group, these offices often provide an extra layer of support. They also are very knowledgeable with regard to financial aid, special opportunities, and social networks especially designed for underrepresented groups.

Although not listed, I wish to mention the following staff members and administrators: Academic Advisors, Transfer Advisors, Peer Mentors, Financial Aid Staff, Department Chair, School Deans, and Student Government Association members.

If you attend a community college, get to know these individuals:

- Transfer/Academic Advisor
- Faculty Member/Instructor
- Administrative Assistants
- Peer Mentors/Leaders
- Student Support Offices
- Multicultural/Special Interest Staff Members
- Financial Aid Workers

A QUICK WORD ABOUT ... STUDENT ATHLETES

If you are a student athlete, your day will be very structured; however, you should try to find the time to form relationships outside of the athletic department. When you are a student athlete, your college experience revolves around the sport that you play. Keep in mind, that your collegiate sports experience will end. You need to plan for your life beyond college sports. Your job is to make sure that you graduate and prepare for the next stage in your life. Although you have to meet many daily demands, you have to at least spend some time in **career services**, so that you can find out what options you have after graduating.

The aforementioned list of people you should know are by no means comprehensive. However, these lists are comprised of the offices and individuals who work very hard to assist students through their academic journey. The college experience is designed to include a team to help you reach success. Everyone at an institution of higher education contributes to your success, whether they are the housekeepers, professors, clerical staff, librarians or the cooks. Just as it takes a village to raise a child, similarly, it takes a institution to graduate a student.

I AM STILL LOST. COULD YOU GIVE ME AN ACTION PLAN?

One great idea in terms of preparing for school is to get your business in order before the first week of classes. When I first arrived at Morgan State University, I made a conscious effort to write out a to-do list that included the people and offices I needed to visit before school started. Creating a to-do list really made my visit more productive and organized. The offices that I visited were the financial aid, **bursar**, and housing office. Additionally, I met with my academic advisor. Taking care of such things the week prior to school proved to be very valuable because when the first day came, I was able to focus on my classes instead of running around campus at the last minute.

A QUICK WORD ABOUT ... PLACEMENT TESTS

At every institution, new students must take a placement test to determine what classes they will be able to take. The general placement tests are typically English/Writing, and Math. Placement tests serve the purpose of helping both you and the institution find the appropriate level of classes for you. Although you may think the tests are unnecessary, they can help you avoid taking a class that could possibly result in failure. The placement test identifies whether or not you need to take developmental (remedial) courses to prepare you for college-level courses. Even if you do not pass the placement test the first time you take it, you can normally retake the test after taking a prerequisite course to help prepare you for future success (check the institution's catalogue for the school's policy). Taking developmental courses and succeeding are important steps to ensuring that you have the skill level necessary for college success.

Once you have taken your placement tests, here is your action plan if you are planning to attend a 4-year institution:

1. **Put forth a vision and set goals:** Success always begins with a vision and stated goals. By setting goals, you will remain focused on what it is you need to do. Ask yourself daily, "Am I moving closer to my goal, or am I regressing?"

2. **Attend orientation:** If there is an **orientation** program offered by your institution, be sure to attend. At most institutions, orientation programs are offered either in the summer or the first week of school. The **Student Activities office** or Student Government Association usually coordinate the orientation program. Orientation is designed to enable you to have a smooth transition into the institution. During orientation, you will have the opportunity to learn about academic and social expectations, meet other students, and learn about the university's services and resources.

3. **Go to the Cashier/Bursar Office:** Be sure that your finances are in order. Pay all of your bills or be sure to secure a payment plan. Also, keep all of your receipts.

4. **Get your student identification card:** At most institutions, the student identification card has multiple purposes. For instance, the university card will allow you access inside your residence hall. Moreover, the card can be used for meal and bookstore purchases. Also, find out what types of student accounts exist. Normally, different student accounts are used to purchase books, meal plans, vending items, and printer and copier usage.

5. **Secure housing:** Be sure to secure your housing. This is something you want to take care of once you make the decision to attend the institution. If you are planning to live on campus, you can contact your Housing or Residence Life office. If you do not plan to live on campus, this office usually has a relationship with landlords off campus. No matter where you choose to live, you will need to fill out a housing application. When filling out a housing application, you will need to pay the application fee and put down a security deposit, present a form of identification (driver's license or student identification card) and provide proof of income (if you are planning to live off campus).

6. **Get your meal plan:** Decide if you want to get a meal plan. If you live on campus, some institutions require you to purchase a meal plan. Before you purchase a meal plan, you should ask if it is required. If you do not ask, the institution may charge you for the meal plan without your consent. Choose a meal plan that best accommodates your eating habits. After all, you can upgrade your meal plan anytime.

7. **Parking:** If possible, before you arrive on campus, you should contact the Parking Services Office (sometimes the office is the same as the campus police office), and get a temporary pass. Also, know ahead of time the parking policies; this may save your car from being towed.

8. **Schedule an appointment with your Academic Advisor:** By meeting with an academic advisor, you can receive help in creating a manageable academic schedule. I suggest that you make your first semester a very light semester so that you have a greater chance of attaining a higher **Grade Point Average (GPA)**. Remember your GPA is very important during your first year. In addition, academic advisors can assign you your **pin number or pass code** so that you can register for your classes online.

9. **Purchase your books:** Find out what books you need before classes start. You can do so by emailing the professor ahead of time. This will save you from a very long line in the bookstore. If you go online to websites like Half.com or Textbooks.com, you can buy your books for a lower price. See appendix B for more information.

10. **Familiarize yourself with various offices:** By familiarizing yourself with various offices, you will become connected with other services, students and staff members.

11. **Locate your classes before the first day:** This will save you time and embarrassment the first day of class. Your RA or another upper-class student can usually help you find your classes. If you are late your first day, you may miss vital information about the course. Typically, all **faculty members** review the syllabus the first day of class. On occasion, professors decide to omit a reading or assignment the first day due to something changing from the time they first drafted the syllabus to the first day of class. Knowing this information is vital to your success.

12. **Meet with a Transfer Counselor:** If you are planning to transfer after the first semester or year, speak with a transfer advisor.

13. **Be excited:** You are about to start on the journey that will transform your life!

If you are planning to attend a community college, here is your action plan:

1. Create a vision and set goals.
2. Attend orientation (if applicable).
3. Go to the Cashier/Bursar Office.
4. Go get your student identification card.
5. Go to Parking Services.
6. Schedule and meet with an academic advisor.
7. Meet with a transfer counselor (if you are planning to transfer).
8. Meet with your academic advisor and schedule/register for your classes.
9. Purchase your books.
10. Familiarize yourself with some of the offices and/or centers.
11. Locate your classes.
12. Be excited!

Note: If you go to the school's website, student handbook, or catalogue, you may find an action plan. In addition, some schools have a central location where you can go to get most of these task completed. However, some things you will have to seek on your own.

I THINK I GOT IT. WHAT OTHER ADVICE SHOULD I KNOW?

In this section, my advice will pertain to lessons that I learned both in college and in life. If you use this advice, it can render major benefits.

TIP #1: Just Stay. When you first arrive on campus, you will probably experience homesickness, however, try not to leave campus too often. The more time you spend getting familiar with the campus and new people, the more it will begin to feel like home.

TIP #2: Take It One Day At A Time. In college, there will be many things happening in your life at once. As a result, expect to have moments where life seems overwhelming. Just take it one day at a time. Find ways to resolve your problems one-step at a time. I suggest creating a to-do list and then designating particular days to get each task completed.

TIP #3: Laws Of The Land. Every campus has its own set of rules and regulations, and they are usually good at letting you know what they are. Restrictions, rules, and regulations of all kinds are found in your student handbook or student code of conduct. The rules are implemented and enforced with the students' best interest in mind. READ THEM.

TIP #4: Know Thy Academic Resources. Taking the time to know where all of the tutorial and computer labs are located (and times they operate) is essential. As you will discover, it matters the most during mid-terms and finals week. Knowing where they all are located and the hours they operate will save you undue stress.

TIP #5: Get A Mentor And Be A Mentor. By definition, a mentor is an individual that is more experienced, who guides and helps another individual. During my first year in college, I was advised early on to adopt a mentor. When I say adopt, I mean find someone to whom you can go for answers, social and professional connections, and if nothing else, encouragement. Mentors come in many forms. They can be campus administrators, staff members, professors, or student leaders. If you find someone with whom you have a strong connection and is more experienced than you are, you may want to consider asking them if they would like to be your mentor. Mentors are sometimes assigned to you and other times you have to seek out the opportunity. If you just simply ask the person if they would like to be your mentor, this will save you the trouble of waiting for a mentor to come along.

You can become a mentor once you graduate or while you are in college. Many institutions have peer-mentoring programs. Having mentors in college really make a difference because they give much needed encouragement during those times when things get tough. They also have the inside track on what it is you need to succeed. Connect with mentors, and then become a mentor yourself!

A QUICK WORD ABOUT ... REFUND CHECKS

A refund is the money left over from your paid balance. If you get more financial aid than the amount of your balance, the institution may owe you some money. If you think that you are due a refund, you should check with both the financial aid office and the bursar/cashier office. There have been students who never picked up their refund checks. Therefore, the institutions have not only saved money but also gained interest from this unclaimed money. Whether you have a refund of $10 or $2000, it is your money!

TIP #6: Adopt Different Mentors. It is advantageous to adopt different types of mentors. First, everyone has different perspectives and experiences to offer. Second, the more mentors you have the more opportunities and social networks you have. Ultimately, it is a good idea to be mentored by people from different cultures than your own and a different gender from yourself.

A QUICK WORD ABOUT ... GAINING FAVOR

If you take the time to get to know people in particular offices, you will gain tremendous favor. I suggest you get to know people in various offices such as the Bursar, Financial Aid, and Special Interest Offices. Also, do not hesitate to do something nice for them in return. I remember on Valentine's Day for two straight years I went to various offices and gave flowers to the women who worked in the offices. Talk about making an impression; I never knew how one kind gesture could go so far. If you think about it, literally hundreds of students walk in and out of offices every semester and while some students may stick out, many go unnoticed.

Even if you do not give them flowers, the little things make a difference. The next time you go into their office or ask them for a favor, they will not only remember you but will be more than willing to help you. One of the highest forms of flattery that I ever received in my life was when one of my students brought me a clock for a graduation gift. Not only did I find the gift flattering but it also proved that she was thankful to have my help. I will never forget her kind gesture, because it reaffirmed my purpose.

"See to do [well], and you will find that happiness will run after you."

—*James Freeman Clarke*

TIP #7: Get Involved In Service Learning Opportunities. At many institutions, service learning not only allows you a chance to give back to the community but also provides you with opportunities to discover your passion or your career. Although students do not typically use these opportunities to network, networking does take place. Many institutions now offer service-learning opportunities for their students.

TIP #8: Attend Institution Sponsored Speeches And Lectures. Institutions usually hire speakers or lecturers as part of a student activities program. By virtue of you paying activity fees, you are paying for these services, whether you take advantage of them or not. You never know what you might learn or what connection you might gain. I knew a student who was looking for an internship and was offered one after attending a lecture series. She was introduced to the speaker after the lecture, was encouraged to exchange information with the speaker, and subsequently, was offered a summer internship!

"Success isn't permanent and failure isn't fatal."

—*Mike Ditka*

TIP #9: Get Involved With Your Major Department. One way to increase your chances of receiving honor society nominations and departmental scholarships is just to be involved with your major department. Your involvement will consistently garner the attention of faculty members and will lead to opportunities.

TIP #10: Look The Part. In an image-conscience society, we are prejudged by our appearance. Many times these prejudgments are wrong. In college, it is no different; if you go to class dressed inappropriately, your classmates and possibly your professor may think differently of you. Instead, if you dress presentably, you will never be questioned in this regard. This does not mean that you have to go to class everyday in a three-piece suit, skirt, or blouse. However, if you dress neatly and cleanly, your perceived appearance will speak of your character, and sometimes your character speaks to what you value. Learning to look the part also helps the transition from college to your career.

A QUICK WORD ABOUT ... STUDY ABROAD PROGRAMS

Perhaps one of my biggest regrets during my undergraduate experience was not participating in a **study abroad** program. If your institution has a study abroad program or international programs office, I highly recommend taking advantage of this opportunity. Besides gaining a greater appreciation of other cultures and a greater global perspective, studying abroad looks very good on your **resume**. Furthermore, you may not have the opportunity to experience such an adventure later in life. If you are unsure whether you will be able to finance this experience, usually the amount that you would normally pay each semester comes close to covering the amount required for the experience. If you receive financial aid and are eligible to receive a **pell grant**, programs like the Benjamin Gillman Scholarship program awards money to students who demonstrate financial need.

TIP #11: It's For Your Own Good. Some students give prerequisites a bad name because they seem to delay graduation. However, prerequisites prepare students for subsequent classes. Think of prerequisites as exhibition games. They may not count toward your record, but they make you better because you build skills and confidence so that you are successful in the future.

TIP #12: Withdraw. If you are failing a class and you know you have no chance at pulling up your grade by midterm, **withdraw** from the class. At most institutions, students are usually allowed to withdraw anytime before midterms. You can withdraw from a class via the internet or by going to the records and **registration** office. Although you may appear to find yourself behind in terms of graduating on time, it makes no sense to stay in a class where you have a strong possibility of failing. If you withdraw from a class, the worse that could happen is that you will need to retake the class. However, if you stay in the class and fail, you will damage your GPA and still have to repeat the course.

TIP #13: Go To A Community College. If you attend a university or college, and if you need to take summer school classes, take summer classes at a community college. The tuition will be much cheaper. However, you will need special permission from your institution. If you are granted permission, you can save a lot of money.

TIP #14: Get A GRE Waiver. At most institutions, if you want to take the GRE (Graduate Records Examination), you can ask for a waiver through the financial aid office. The GRE is a test that is required for most postgraduate programs. Generally, you can receive a waiver if you are receiving financial aid. The best time to inquire about a waiver is at the beginning of the school year, as the money used for this waiver is still available.

TIP #15: Get On The School's Listserve. If you are unsure about activities that may be happening on your campus, ask to be placed on the Student Activities, student organization, or department's lists serve.

TIP #16: Take Responsibility. In high school you probably had the benefit of teachers calling your house if you missed a few days of class. However, in college if you do not attend class, the professors will not call home. In college, you are considered an adult. Part of being an adult is learning to be accountable for your actions.

Although you may read this book in the very beginning of your journey, the information can be applied throughout your college experience. As previously stated, it is not enough to get into college. Ultimately, it is about having good experiences throughout your college experience and graduating.

Chapter Three

What about The Academic Experience of College?

"If you love what you do, you won't work a day in your life."

—*Unknown*

"Nothing is particularly hard if you divide it into small jobs."

—*Henry Ford*

QUESTIONS THAT THIS CHAPTER WILL COVER:

1. I am not sure I know how to study for college. Could you give me some study tips?
2. I hear college is about time management. Can you give me some time management tips?
3. I hear professors are out to get students. Is that true?
4. How do I choose a major?

In college, your full-time job is being a college student. For some, this is the part of college that is extremely difficult. Make no mistake; college should be a fun time. However, it is also a time to focus on learning and establishing the skills necessary for you to move forward in life. Whether you were a straight A student in high school or a below average student, it does not matter anymore. This is a new beginning and with a new beginning comes new challenges and opportunities. If you take the time to develop relationships with your professors and utilize your resources, it is impossible to fail. In this chapter, I will provide tips to assist you throughout your academic journey.

I AM NOT SURE I KNOW HOW TO STUDY FOR COLLEGE. COULD YOU GIVE ME SOME STUDY TIPS?

"If you study to remember, you will forget, but, if you study to understand, you will remember."

—Unknown

Some of the best advice that I received about becoming a better student was finding a plan that worked for me. No one knows you like you know yourself. You know what time of day you like to study and under what conditions. As you go along in college, you will learn more about yourself. In the meantime, here are some study tips that can help you become a better student:

TIP #1: Be Flexible. Although you do not always have control over what comes your way, you always have control over how you respond. For that matter, do not expect things to always go your way. For this reason alone, there are few things in life that are truly life and death.

TIP #2: Know Your Place. If you are having difficulty in reading, you should find a comfortable location and choose a regular reading place and time. In all of my years of college, I never knew a student who had the same regular place; you just have to find what works for you. For some students, their place is the library, and for others, their room is their best choice.

TIP #3: Get Started. Get started with your homework in spite of whether you like it or not. Once you start, you may find it easier to continue. I have found this especially true for writing papers. Every person has days when he or she cannot seem to get started doing something, but the key is that you start. When it comes to writing papers, motivation can come and go. The hardest part is just getting started.

> "Happiness does not depend on outward things, but on the way we see them."
>
> *—Count Leo Tolstoy, Russian novelist*

TIP #4: Try To Study Daily. The best strategy is to study daily! In high school, you could probably study the day before an exam and still do well. This is not the correct approach in college, although many students still try this approach. This is especially helpful in those subjects in which you might struggle. Know your weaknesses, and manage your time accordingly. One hour does make a difference although it may not seem that way. In college, no one is telling you when and how to study, so it is up to you to devote the time to study.

TIP #5: Break It Up. If you have a hard time concentrating, take short, beneficial breaks. Studies suggest that the average human attention span is only about 20 minutes at a time. Therefore, if you took 5-minute breaks for every 20 minutes, this will help you refocus and concentrate better. Set a goal of reading a certain amount of pages or completing a certain number of problems. When you have accomplished your goal, reward yourself by taking a break and doing something you enjoy. Think of things you like to do and make them incentives. Remain focused while you study. The more you find yourself not going somewhere with something, the more you will waste your time. If you can only focus for one hour, then focus for one hour, and take a break.

TIP #6: A City Is Not Built Overnight. Nothing worth doing is done overnight. The same applies for what you do in school. If you approach studying by breaking the job up in small tasks in order to complete the assignment, you will be amazed at how efficient you will become. If you try to take on the entire task, you will become overwhelmed and may achieve nothing. Everything has a process.

TIP #7: Minimize Multi-Tasking. In a world where multi-tasking is very much a part of our culture, it might be beneficial to minimize some of the multi-tasking when you need to concentrate. This should ensure that you are more concentrated on the project. If you are having major trouble concentrating on your work, it can be worthwhile to consult a doctor. Sometimes undiagnosed medical conditions can go unnoticed.

> "Learn the art of converting failure into success and challenge into opportunity. There is no failure for the person who has mastered this art."
>
> —*Unknown*

TIP #8: Do The Easy Part First. Sometimes if you do the easy part first, it may give you motivation to continue. I found this to be helpful with math and science. By doing the easy part first, it puts you in a rhythm and once you catch a rhythm, it is much easier to stay focused on what must be done.

> "Anything worth doing is worth doing poorly until you learn to do it well."
>
> —*Steve Brown*

TIP #9: Be Selective In Your Reading. If you want to be quicker with your reading, keep in mind that only some material is worth studying, and the rest is just worth skimming. Begin by skimming through the table of contents, introduction, conclusion, and key chapters. Also, read the first and last paragraphs of each chapter. This will give you a sense of the overall theme of the reading and its main points.

TIP #10: Focus On and Mark Key Points. As you read, focus on key points and mark them. When you go back, it can serve as a quick reference. This can be accomplished by using asterisks and highlighting sentences.

TIP #11: Study With A Friend. Enlist a friend and study the subject together. However, by all means, study with someone who can help you with the subject. Sometimes we hinder ourselves more by adding more distractions.

TIP #12: Proofread Backward. When you are assigned a written essay and everything needs to be spelled correctly, read your paper backward. This process will help you not to skip over words.

TIP #13: Build Your Vocabulary. Before you start reading, decide beforehand that you will read five or ten pages before you take a break. After you have marked the pages, briefly go through the contents and underline the words that you do not understand. After you have done this, look up the meanings of no more than ten words. Write down the meanings in your notebook, and look up the meanings of the other words in your next study session.

TIP #14: Record Yourself. If you want to memorize something, record yourself, and then listen to yourself saying it repeatedly. If you are practicing a speech or presentation, you can also ask friends to video tape you so you can see your body gestures and language while you talk.

TIP #15: Know Your Learning Style. There are usually three types of learners: visual, audio, and tactile. If you are having trouble figuring out your learning style or if you just do not know where to begin, go to the career or counseling center and take an assessment. Kolb's Learning Style Inventory is one such assessment inventory. Also, remember that study techniques are very subjective: What might work for your friend might not work for you and vice versa. If you are assessed during your first semester of college, you will benefit greatly from the results.

> "Don't bother just to be better than your contemporaries or predecessors. Try to be better than yourself."
>
> —*William Faulkner*

TIP #16: Form Study Groups. If you are struggling in a particular subject, ask a group of classmates to join you in forming a study group. Study groups are great because you can quiz each other, divide sections, and become experts in specific sections.

TIP#17: Anticipate Exam Questions. This is very important for many exams, especially for essay exams. Upon writing down possible questions, write out the answers prior to the exam and memorize the main points. By doing this, when you get to similar questions on the exam, you will not be easily rattled. Consequently, you will not take up a lot of time trying to write an answer.

TIP#18: Reorganize Your Notes. If your handwriting is as bad as mine, rewrite your notes within a day in order to organize and expand the information. If you wait too long, you may not remember the details later. Moreover, rewriting your notes is an excellent study tool to help you remember the information.

"Help others achieve their dreams and you will achieve yours."

—*Les Brown*

TIP#19: Take It Easy. When taking an exam, answer the easier questions first and save the harder questions for later. This will save you a great deal of time so that you can focus your attention on the part of the exam that is most challenging. This will also help reduce anxiety and stress. By taking care of the easy questions first, you at least know that you will get some right.

TIP #20: Utilize Tutorial Services. Someone once told me that if I did not go see the tutor for help, the tutor still got paid. In most cases, if no one visits, the tutor socializes with others or works on their own homework. This is a fact. I had many tutors in college because of all of my difficulties in math and science. Although I still had to work hard, the tutors helped to make the concepts easier to understand. One thing is certain, whenever I made the point to keep regular appointments with a tutor, I never failed a test, and I never had to repeat a class. The lesson here is clear: When in college, do not be afraid to ask for help!

I HEAR COLLEGE IS ABOUT TIME MANAGEMENT. CAN YOU GIVE ME SOME TIME MANAGEMENT TIPS?

"It's a dream until you write it down, and then it's a goal."

—*Anonymous*

"Worrying is like a rocking chair: it gives you something to do, but it doesn't get you anywhere."

—*Unknown*

Let me begin by defining time management and what it means in college. Time management is how you go about regulating and scheduling your time. The key to successful time management is using your time efficiently to balance and complete your academic, personal, and social goals. Additionally, it is finding time to take advantage of all of the opportunities that will help you grow and develop. Listed below are time management tips that will help you stay organized and focused.

TIP #1: Set Daily And Weekly Goals. Once you have a sense of direction, you will have a sense of purpose and tasks will seem more meaningful. When you set daily and weekly goals, it allows you to see the progress that you have made over time. Additionally, connect daily and weekly goals with long-term goals. For example, if your goal for the semester is to lose ten pounds, you may wish to go to the gym three times a week. Having structure keeps you focused.

"The quality of a person's life is in direct proportion to their commitment to excellence."

—*Vince Lombardi*

TIP #2: Do Not Forget To Take Time For You. It is okay to say no. If you do not have the energy to help yourself, how can you help others?

TIP #3: Do Not Procrastinate. Time is your most valuable resource. Procrastinating is something that we all are guilty of doing. However, if procrastination is not placed in check, it can come back to haunt you. Choose your time wisely, and remember you must get things done eventually. On the other hand, if you complete your task early, you have more time to correct last minute mistakes. If you wait until the last minute, that time is no longer available.

TIP #4: Prioritize Your Time. So many new things exist to do at a new college or university. It is important to become involved with campus life and make friends, but do not forget why you are in school. Find ways to manage your time and figure out what is most important.

TIP #5: Be Intentional. Explore new ideas and discover how they relate to you, but do not make decisions too fast. Most decisions are better when they are planned out. Some of the choices you make in college could continue to affect you for the rest of your life. For instance, if you choose to take out a student loan to pay for an expensive car (I have heard stories about this), you will eventually have to pay back the loan. Although sometimes it may be hard to imagine what life will be like years from now, that day does eventually come along.

A QUICK WORD ABOUT ... SUCCESS

Success can mean different things to different people. Your success depends on what your expectations are and how you go about trying to achieve that goal. For example, one student passed a test with a C and, in doing so; he passed the class after taking it for a second time. Another student passed the class with a C after taking it for the first time. Which student was successful? Success depended upon what each student hoped to achieve prior to taking the class. The student who made the C after taking the class for a second time found success. For this student, success meant not to fail the class again. However, the other student who passed the class the first time with a C was disappointed because he thought that he could make an A instead of a C in the class. Therefore, the first student felt successful while the second student felt unsuccessful.

Success is all about perception and expectation. In order to be successful in college, you must make realistic goals that are both measurable and achievable. If you set unrealistic goals, you will be disappointed every time. On the other hand, if you set goals that are measurable and achievable, you find success in the smallest of victories. You are not today who you will be tomorrow. Give yourself time to grow and develop. Learn from your mistakes and do not forget to celebrate your small accomplishments.

I HEAR PROFESSORS ARE OUT TO GET STUDENTS. IS THAT TRUE?

"A man's mind, once stretched by a new idea, never regains its original dimensions."

—*Oliver Wendell Holmes*

Professors, teaching assistants, course instructors, and other faculty members all have the distinct privilege of teaching college students. At first, these professionals may seem a bit intimidating; however, once you get to know them, you will discover that they are just regular people. College teachers can serve as great mentors and can connect with you in unimaginable ways. From one who has developed great friendships with professors, I can assure you that getting to know your professors will bring positive results, especially if later in the semester you run into some problems. Remember, they want to help, not hinder you. You just have to make the effort to meet them halfway. Below are a few tips I found useful when communicating and working with college educators.

TIP #1: Form a Relationship With Your Professors. In addition to helping to clarify course material and assignments, professors can be a source of networking contacts. In addition, they can write letters of recommendations. They want to see you succeed more than you might imagine. No professor I have met wanted students to fail and be miserable!

TIP #2: If Your Professor Is Running Late, Stick Around. There is a college rumor out there that if a professor is running 15 minutes late for class, you are at liberty to leave. I have never read this in a college catalogue. Furthermore, I do not believe that leaving is in your best interest. I advise you to stay even if a professor is running late. Should you decide to stay, this will convey three possible messages to your professor. First, you are deeply interested in the course or topic of that day. Second, you are committed to your education. Third, you are respectful of your professor's time. The professor will most likely make a mental note of your choice, especially if you are one of few who stayed. If you are struggling in the course, the good impression you make on the professor by choosing to stay may make the difference between an A or B or pass or fail grade.

TIP #3: Survey the Class Beforehand. Always learn more about the instructor and course prior to registering for the class. You can do so by obtaining a copy of the syllabus from the previous semester. Often times, this can be accomplished by searching the school's Website. Additionally, there are Websites such as www.ratemyprofessor.com. Furthermore, find out what circumstances are happening in the professor's life. For example, I had a professor once who was in the dissertation phase of her doctorate program. As a result, she was spending a lot of her time and energy to complete her dissertation. Although she had a reputation for being a tough grader, and students normally had to work hard to make an A in her class, she eased up on her requirements so that she would have time to spend on her dissertation. While she still presented challenging material, there was a noticeable difference in her course assignments during that semester. Needless to say, the semester in which I took the class was the best time to take her class. I could focus more of my attention on doing really well in other classes in which I struggled.

TIP #4: Know Your Course Load. This tip is not necessarily a tip for working with professors; however, I think it is a rule that every student should learn the first semester. One of the lessons that I learned during college was not to take all extremely challenging classes in one semester. Rather, figure out early on what you have to take and figure how best to arrange your courses. For example, if you know that English and history are your difficult subjects, take one of these classes and complement it with two classes that seem more manageable. By planning the semester this way, your confidence, sanity, and most importantly, your GPA should not suffer. Eventually you will have to take the hard classes, but by that time, you will have figured out how to navigate through college, which includes knowing where to go for help. For example, if you start with a high GPA your first semester and you have an awful GPA the next semester, you will still be in good standing. However, if you start with a bad GPA and continue this bad streak, you may be in jeopardy of academic probation, which can result in losing financial aid or being asked to leave the institution.

TIP #5: Take Advantage Of Office Hours. If ever you are unclear on an assignment or just want to speak with your instructor, schedule a time to meet them during office hours. Your professor will designate office hours in which they will be available to discuss class-related issues. In my experience, this was the time that I received clarity about assignments and tests. Additionally, this was a time that I formed a relationship with the professor so that I stood out from the rest of my peers. Though it may seem like "butt kissing," it pays to get to know your instructors. Again, knowing your professors personally could very well mean the difference in a letter grade. In the least, knowing your professors will provide you with fantastic mentors.

TIP #6: Turn In Assignments Early. Some professors will allow you to turn in your assignment a couple of days early so that they can look them over. However, some professors will not offer this service. If this is the case, then you should speak with your professor about this matter. By turning in assignments early, you show the professor two very important things: You want to do well in their class and you are well prepared.

A QUICK WORD ABOUT ... ADDING AND DROPPING CLASSES

At the beginning of the semester, you will have the opportunity to **add** and/or **drop** classes. This usually is an option during the first week. When adding or dropping classes, figure out if that class is going to work in your schedule. Before you add or drop a class, ask yourself what you are hoping to accomplish by adding/dropping this class. Do you need to take this class immediately? How does this fit into your structure of classes? In other words, is it worth taking the risk? If you know that this class will probably overwhelm you along with other classes that you will be taking, it is probably a good idea to drop the class and pick it up later. On the other hand, if you know that you can handle an extra class, you could get it out of the way. Before adding or dropping a class, be sure to find out what the specifics are at your institution. You can usually obtain this information from the catalogue, student handbook, Website, or your academic advisor.

TIP #7: Visit Your Professors. If you and the professor have made a good connection the previous semester, continue to keep in touch. Often times opportunities cross their desk that can benefit you. As previously stated, if you establish a relationship with your professor, they will always keep you in mind when opportunities arise. Always stay visible whether through email or by visits to their office.

TIP #8: Preview Readings. If you preview the reading before class, you will have a better understanding of what the professor is talking about before class starts.

TIP #9: Ask For Extra Credit. Some professors will pre-assign extra credit in the beginning of the semester, while others will not. Sometimes if you just ask, professors will be more than willing to assign extra credit. A good strategy is to ask the first day of class with the support of your fellow classmates. In this case, they may feel more compelled to give extra credit because the entire class is making the request. The worst thing that can happen is for a professor to say no. In spite of this, the professor will more than likely remember who you are (which makes you the ultimate winner).

HOW DO I CHOOSE A MAJOR?

"The only path that is right for you is the one your heart tells you to follow."

—Unknown

Someone asked me a long time ago, "Tawan, what do you love to do?" The person also followed up with the question, "If you could do anything for free, what would you do?" For a very long time, this question stifled me. "I really am not sure," I replied at the time. When the questions were posed to me, I was more concerned with making money as opposed to finding something that I really loved. As time went on, fortunately I learned more about myself and found my passion. Too often, we all make the mistake of pursuing a degree because it pays good money. The day you decide to focus on what you love to do and not on how much money you will make will be the day that your life forever changes.

I know it is not easy when you have loans to pay or when you are short of cash; nevertheless, as a friend once told me, go for what you love to do, and the money will eventually follow. It is hard to see that truth when you are just beginning. Deciding on a career choice is of course one of the hardest things to figure out in college. Obviously, you have not had enough time to figure out who you are let alone what you want to do for the rest of your life. You need time to discover what career will excite you. However, if someone is paying for your education, they may not want to hear that you need extra time in college because you have not figured out what you want to do with your life yet. College is expensive, but being miserable with a rushed career choice is more expensive.

TIP #1: When Changing Majors, Do Not Feel Discouraged. There have been and will always be thousands of students to change their major throughout college. You are not alone. It is more important to find out what interests you now then declaring a major only to regret it later. The best thing about changing your major several times is that you are taking the time to discover who you are and where you want to be. This process of discovery may be time consuming but what will be even more time consuming is going to work everyday, hating what you do, and finally realizing that the job you have is not for you.

TIP #2: Take An Inventory. When exploring potential majors you should spend time getting to know yourself, your abilities, and your motivations. The first task that I suggest for you is to go to the Career Services office and take a career assessment. This will help you better understand what types of jobs or careers appeal to you. This service usually is underutilized, but it can be very beneficial. Visit your career services office as soon as you can. Additionally, ask yourself the following questions:

- What are my strengths?
- What are my weaknesses?
- What would I do for free? What do I really enjoy?
- What skills do I possess?
- What were my best subjects in high school?
- What extracurricular activities did I participate in the past?
- What skills did I learn from part-time or summer jobs?
- What things do I value in life?
- What do I value in a job or career?
- What are some other resources for helping me get more information about a major and/or a career?

A QUICK WORD ABOUT ... INTERNSHIPS

Internships are experiences for students to combine a career-related work experience with academic coursework. Most internships are worked during the summer; however, depending upon the internship, you can work it during the school year.

If you go to the career services office in a timely manner, you may be able to secure an internship. Additionally, staff members will give you interviewing tips and help you create your resume. In addition, begin looking for an internship around October or November. Many students make the mistake of looking for an internship at the beginning of the summer or late April. By this time, the internship opportunities are usually no longer available. As the saying goes, the early bird gets the worm. Finding internships are all about preparation, patience, and persistence. Furthermore, because some internships require recommendations, be sure to enlist people who can provide you with *favorable* recommendations early.

TIP #3: Take A Variety Of Classes. By taking a variety of classes, you will get a better feel for what you really like and what you really dislike. During my first and second year of college, I took a variety of classes that allowed me to get to know what I did not like. In any case, do not select a major until you are fully sure what you want to do. Take a variety of classes your first year because this is the time to explore what you want to do. Choosing a college major is a process just like selecting a school to attend.

"Man cannot discover new oceans until he has the courage to lose the sight of land."

—*Unknown*

TIP #4: Find Your Passion. When I saw the movie *Office Space*, it made me think of this point. Some people spend the majority of their adult lives working a job that they hate for a living. As a result, they never feel good about going to work each day. Find the thing that makes you happy (no matter how it sounds to others) because your life depends on it. It is not about the money, and it is not about what others think. Instead, it is about how you want to live your life every day. Therefore, do not feel pressured to make a hasty decision about selecting a career or a major. It does not matter if it seems as though everyone else knows what they plan to do with their life—believe me; they don't.

A QUICK WORD ABOUT ... BAD GRADES AND WHAT CAN BE LEARNED

The grade you receive in a class does not reflect your intelligence. In addition, grades do not necessarily reflect what you learned or how hard you worked. While grades matter a great deal, if you fail a class, it is not the end of the world. Despite failing three classes in college, I still graduated with a high GPA. From this experience, I discovered that the bad grades were not a testament of my intelligence or abilities. Instead, the grades were a testament to how well I managed my study time and how much effort I really put forth in the class. In some instances, the bad grade was proof that the subject matter held little interest for me. One of the lessons that I learned after switching my major for the second time was to listen to my intuition. For instance, if you know in your heart that you want to become a teacher, then become a teacher. Listen to your instincts, and you will find a much more fulfilling career.

"Success is getting up one more time than you fall down."

—Unknown

TIP #7: Get To Know Upper-Class Students. By getting to know upper-class students you have access to a wealth of information that is readily available. These students have often already encountered what you are about to experience. Hence, they may know of opportunities that you have not explored.

TIP #8: Go Elsewhere. If your institution does not offer an adequate career services center, then you should check out a career services center at a nearby institution or local library. In most cases, staff members will still assist you even if you are not a student at their institution.

"The world does not pay for what a person knows. But it pays for what a person does with what he knows."

—Laurence Lee

In conclusion, choosing a major, getting to know your professors, and developing good study and time management habits are vital to your success. Take the time to get to know who you are. Do not become so focused on finishing school that you fail to discover what career will make you happy. College is the time for you to discover who you are, what you enjoy doing, what you are good at doing, and what you want to be. Choosing a career is not a race; take your time and enjoy exploring your options. Moreover, do not worry; the money will come eventually. In thirty years, if you can say that you have accomplished everything that you wanted to do, then taking the time to get through school will have been well worth it, no matter how long it took you. Without having a sense of who you are and in what direction you want to go, you may find yourself wasting your time and money or worse, not living up to your full potential.

Chapter Four

What about The Social Experience of College?

"All work and no play makes Jack a dull boy; but all play and no work makes him something greatly worse."

—*Samuel Smiles*

"Don't let someone else's opinion of you become your reality."

—*Les Brown*

QUESTIONS COVERED IN THIS CHAPTER:

1. I am concerned about forming and losing relationships with family and friends. What advice can you offer about my family and friends?

2. I am too busy to exercise; do you have any advice about staying fit while in college?

3. What kinds of things can I get involved with outside of the classroom?

4. I Have Heard Many Interesting Things about College. Is It All True? If So, What Can I Do About It?

For some people, college is a time to party and get away with things that would be deemed unacceptable later in life. These same people would probably argue that it is a time of experimentation. For others, college is a time to lay down the foundation for their future. For them, it is a time to make a decision about the kind of life they want to live. College should certainly be a fun time in your life because you have the benefits of being an adult but not necessarily all of the responsibility. However, remember that you are there to accomplish a larger goal.

A QUICK WORD ABOUT ... LEARNING IN COLLEGE

Learning on a college campus takes many forms and takes place in various settings. The settings for these learning opportunities may take place in the residence hall, student union, and even the dining hall. The truth is that many of the experiences that students encounter outside of the classroom are always opportunities for growth and development. Conversations, debates, conflicts, and confrontations are all ways that learning can be experienced. Learning is transformative and can be experienced anywhere. Whatever form or setting it might be, take advantage of the opportunities presented. Be proactive when you approach learning and don't limit learning to just the classroom.

I AM CONCERNED ABOUT FORMING AND LOSING RELATIONSHIPS WITH FAMILY AND FRIENDS. WHAT ADVICE CAN YOU OFFER ABOUT MY FAMILY AND FRIENDS?

"Adversity introduces a man to himself."

—Unknown

TIP #1: Different Friends For Different Reasons. One of the things that I found helpful in going through college, particularly in graduate school, was finding people who had multiple purposes. You will have different types of friends: those with whom you party, those with whom you study, those with whom you hang out, and those to whom you tell your deepest and darkest secrets. Find different friends for different things and do not ever expect or assume that you can receive all things from just one person. If you do, you will be deeply disappointed every time. I have had friends make the mistake of trying to make their significant other fit into their every interest. The clear problem with this situation is that when the two separated, they suddenly had no other friends outside of their relationship because they spent so much time together. So do yourself a favor and find a diverse group of friends.

> "Difficulties in your life do not come to destroy you, but to help you to realize your hidden potentials. So let difficulties know that YOU are difficult."
>
> *—Unknown*

TIP #2: Roommate Issues. As a live-in staff member at three different institutions, I have mediated many roommate conflicts. What I have discovered, in most cases, is that the conflicts have stemmed from making assumptions that resulted from one person not expressing how they felt about something or not being clear about expectations in the beginning. You do not have to be best friends with your roommate. If it does not work out, it is perfectly okay. Remember, you are never trapped in a situation. Most institutions have emergency housing for students who may be in some kind of accommodation. The person who should know about your roommate issues should be your Resident Assistant (RA) or the RA's supervisor, because no one else can really assist you like they can. Not every one is meant to live together.

TIP #3: Not Everyone Feels The Same. Use your family and friends as support but realize that everyone is not always going to understand your excitement and thus will not be as excited about your accomplishments as you will be. Sometimes family members are not excited for you because they just don't understand. I remember receiving a prestigious award and sharing this great news with my family. To my surprise, my family did not seem as excited about the achievement as I had anticipated. I remember being upset because in my opinion, this achievement was a big deal. From that day forward, I learned a very valuable lesson: Be understanding.

TIP #4: Change Takes Change. Leaving a friend behind is one of the hardest things you can do. However, if the relationship is meant to last, it will last. Many people go away to college thinking their old friendships will remain the same. However, the day you set foot on a college campus, things are more than likely to change. Remember that change is apart of life. You may have friends back home who will still expect you to be the same person when you return home. They may say to you that you have changed, and they are probably right. Do not be afraid of change. You have to welcome the possibilities that come with change. The best part about college is that you have the opportunity to meet many different kinds of people with whom you can learn and grow.

"No one can make you feel inferior without your own consent."

—Eleanor Roosevelt

TIP #5: Learn To Say No. In college, every week presents different challenges, so you must stay focused. When friends stop by, do not be afraid to say no if you have homework or other deadlines. More often than not, many other occasions will arise when you will have time to spend with them. However, you may not have another occasion to complete the assignment. As difficult as it may be, your academics have to be the priority.

A QUICK WORD ABOUT … DIVERSITY

No matter what school you decide to attend, you can always expect to find diversity on a college campus. Even though diversity is often thought of in terms of external features—ethnicity, age, and appearance, diversity is so much more. Along with things like sexual orientation, socioeconomic status, ethnicity, and gender, diversity can be defined in terms of beliefs, values, thoughts, and learning abilities. Consequently, although people may share the same ethnicity or gender, no one person is the same. While I cannot tell you how to feel about anyone or any particular group, I can tell you that diversity is not going to go away. In fact, our world is shrinking due to the explosion of technology. We are a global community now. Therefore, the sooner that everyone realizes this, the sooner we can learn to better understand each other.

TIP #6: People Come And People Go. It is a natural part of life for people to come and go. I remember once in college being distraught over a relationship that had turned bad and my mentor told me that when one door closes, another door opens. He went on to say that this will not be the last time I encounter a situation like this one. It will only make me stronger and more prepared for the next time. The reason that I share this story is to say that people come in your life for a reason, season, and lifetime. We have to be able to recognize which category people fit into and be okay with the reality of the situation. In your first semester, you may think that you have found your best friend forever; however, by the end of the college experience, you may end up feeling differently about that person. In any case, do not be afraid to let go because letting go is the only way we can make room for new experiences.

TIP #7: Beliefs Change. While attending college, your opinions about many things will inevitably change. For some, these changes occur the first semester, while for others, these changes occur more gradually. Your beliefs will change as you mature. College allows you to discover that there are multiple truths and that learning is an ongoing process.

TIP #8: Situations Arise. When situations arise, let someone know who can help you do something about it. If you just talk to your family or friends about the situation and you do not go beyond talking with the person with whom you are having problems, you will never find a solution. Sometimes the person has no idea what is wrong until you bring it to their attention. Many arguments and misunderstandings stem from miscommunication. Although other people can help assist you in a situation, you must first help yourself.

> "Stay positive, live positive, surround yourself around positive people and positive things and you will succeed."
>
> —*Sal A. Betancourt*

I AM TOO BUSY TO EXERCISE; DO YOU HAVE ANY ADVICE ABOUT STAYING FIT WHILE IN COLLEGE?

> "We either make ourselves happy or miserable. The amount of work is the same."
>
> —*Carlos Castaneda, Peruvian-American mystic and author*

Staying fit while in college can be a challenge. If you are like every other college student, you are trying to find balance in your life. You have exams, scholarly projects, homework, extracurricular activities, work, and other commitments. On top of all of this, you have to find ways to make sure you stay healthy. I know how hard it is to find a healthy balance in college. Whether your concern is to keep off the weight or to minimize stress, staying healthy in college should be a top priority.

TIP #1: Learn About The Symptoms Of Stress. I do not want to give you more homework than you already have; however, learning about the symptoms of stress can help you better assess when you are pushing yourself too hard or when you become too overwhelmed. Stress can kill you. There is no other way to put it. Stress can lead to obesity, depression, insomnia, anxiety, alcohol and drug abuse. However, there is good news. Stress is not permanent. You can reduce or even eliminate stress by finding manageable ways to deal with it. One of my suggestions is to exercise on a regular basis. It does not matter what form of exercise you decide upon as long as you exercise regularly. I remember taking a weight lifting class just to have exercise built into my schedule. Not only was the class an easy A, but also it was a great way to ensure that I was exercising regularly.

TIP #2: You Are What You Eat. When you eat food in a dining hall, you are eating food that is prepared for everybody on campus. For example, colleges and universities use processed foods and they do not take into consideration any dietary needs or other concerns. Dining halls try to offer healthy choices, but quantity usually takes precedence over quality. So, watch what you eat.

TIP #3: Do Not Eat Late At Night. When you get the munchies, you want to eat. If you want to gain weight in college, the best way to do it is to eat unhealthy late-night meals and snacks. I remember gaining roughly 15 pounds in one semester from eating late nearly every night. If you do decide to eat out and/or late at night, do it in moderation.

Here are some tips to help you maintain a healthy college lifestyle:

- **Exercise late at night.** If you exercise later in the night after you eat, you will work off the extra calories.
- **Brush your teeth.** By brushing your teeth when you get the urge to munch, you will be less likely to snack late at night.
- **Eat fiber.** Eating foods like oatmeal will make you feel fuller and curb your appetite.
- **Walk.** If you live on a large campus that utilizes public transportation, take a walk instead of using the transit system. Since your destination will be farther away, you will be sure to exercise every day.

- **Have other options.** If you know you are a late-night snacker, grab healthy snacks earlier in the day when your options are more abundant. For example, grab an apple at lunch and save it for later.

- **Join an intramural club.** By joining an intramural club, you compete against other teams. When you compete, you usually have a reason to stay in shape. After all, two of the biggest motivators in life are games and competition.

TIP #4: Wash Up. Having good hygiene is the best way to stay healthy at school. Taking a shower daily (it is not as common as you think) will minimize germs and bacteria. In addition, it will make you feel much better.

TIP #5: Get Spiritual. Looking back, college was a lot easier when I took the time to adjust my spiritual well-being. It is a well-known fact that spirituality is very important in staying healthy in college. I am not advocating any particular spiritual belief. However, attending to your spiritual well-being is just as important as attending to your physical, mental, and emotional well-being. What you believe is not as important as realizing that spiritual well being is also an important part of staying healthy in college.

TIP #6: Get Some Rest. Sleep is perhaps the most important part of staying healthy because without a good night's rest, we cannot be alert or at our very best. Therefore, find a time for sleep that works for you. If you do not sleep at a reasonable hour in the night, take a nap during the day (not in class). Taking a "power nap" will at least energize you during the day.

WHAT KINDS OF THINGS CAN I GET INVOLVED WITH OUTSIDE OF THE CLASSROOM?

"It takes a whole village to raise a child."

—*Ashanti proverb*

During my first two years of high school, I was not a particularly good student. I guess I always had potential, but I never got excited about school. This all changed when I began to participate in after school activities. Extracurricular school activities, in particular student organizations, made me really feel good about school. In fact, my grades were much better when I was involved in extra-curricular activities.

Basic student services offered by most institutions include student health services, advising and counseling, and academic support services (centers established by the university to help students with various subjects, such as English, math, science, etc.). No matter what your needs may be, your school probably offers organizations that will interest you or can help you. The school registers and sponsors some organizations, while students run others. Typically, if you cannot find a student organization that fits your needs, you can start your own organization. You can create your own organization by writing your own constitution and bylaws, registering your organization with the Student Government Association or Student Activities office, and petitioning for membership. Every institution has a different process of activating organizations. It is very important that you find your social group in an institution because this group will give you another reason to stay in college.

Here is a list of the common student support offices that you should utilize:

Academic or Learning Centers
Campus Ministry or Religious Services
Career Services
Counseling Center
Disability Services
Health Center
International Education and Study Abroad Office
Multicultural Affairs
Office of Residence Life/Housing
Student Activities
Student Employment Office
Student Government Association
Student Support Services Offices
Tutorial Centers

A QUICK WORD ABOUT ... OVER INVOLVEMENT

As with anything in life, too much of a good thing can be a bad thing. During my final year of college, I found myself overcommitted in many of my student leadership roles. So much, that at times it seemed like I was a college administrator and not a student. As a student leader, you will receive many benefits for being involved in student organizations, but you can also find yourself losing your focus or not fully enjoying your college experience.

Campus Administrators ask the same group of students to participate in activities as opposed to taking the time to find other potential student leaders. In many cases, this is because these student leaders are visible and to a large degree, very outspoken. Being overly committed in student activities can be just as unhealthy as partying too much. Although you may be a member of every organization on campus, are you really committing yourself to your academics and taking care of yourself? Balance and moderation is the key. Remain focused on your larger goal, and learn to prioritize. If you were a member of ten organizations and you received every student leadership award, what good is it really, if you never graduate?

BECOME A RESIDENT ASSISTANT

"Help others get ahead. You will always stand taller with someone else on your shoulders."

—*Bob Moawad*

Another way to become involved while you live on campus is by becoming a Resident Assistant (RA). Upon transferring from community college, I wanted to join the track team for the university. At the time, it seemed like a very good idea because it was something that I always wanted to do. However, I also wanted to explore other student leadership roles. After having a conversation with my RA, (who also ran track) he told me that if I am looking just to stay in shape, run track but if I am looking for doors to open beyond college then become an RA. The following year I decided to become RA. Little did I know how much this decision would significantly influence my career path. Before I explain the benefits of being an RA, it is important for me to tell you what Resident Assistants do. A RA is a student leader who lives on the floor in a residence hall or other campus housing with other students. They are responsible for building community, organizing social and education activities, crisis intervention, and enforcing university and hall policies. Many schools have different names for the position. Some of these terms include Resident Advisor, Community Assistant, Community Advisor, Senior Resident, and Floor Fellow. Some of the skills that RAs gain are crisis management, mediation, and event planning skills.

While this may sound like a lot of work, the benefits of being an RA far exceed the work that may be involved. Some of the monetary benefits of being an RA usually include free room and board. At some institutions, in addition to room and board, the RA receives a small stipend, and summer employment. Aside from the tangible benefits, RAs receive leadership training and experience that they can list on their resume. They also are a vital part of a student's development and learning. Because RAs serve on the front line, they can have the biggest impact on a student's life. Their role is crucial because they often become the peers to whom students often feel safe to talk about their frustrations, accomplishments, and problems. For example, when I served as an RA in college, a resident tearfully confided in me about his situation with his girlfriend that had gone downhill. At that moment, I was the most important person in his life because I was there in his time of need. Although he and I never really spoke about this situation again, I knew that he was grateful for the conversation we had that night.

Another benefit to being an RA is the opportunity to go to graduate school at a reduced cost. In fact, many people have used this opportunity as a means to pay for graduate school. If you have been an RA and you want to continue a similar experience in graduate school, you can become a Resident Director or **Assistant Resident Director (ARD)** and have the university pay for your education. In most instances, if you serve as a Residence Director, the university will pay for your tuition, provide you with housing, and give you a salary or stipend. The compensation package varies from institution to institution, but there is some form of compensation. It is one of the most well-kept secrets for paying for graduate school. The best place to look for this type of opportunity is the university's housing or residence life website. In my opinion, no other student leadership experience rivaled my experience as an RA. If you are interested in being an RA, you can go to the appendix at the back of this book for more information. Also, speak with your RA.

In addition to being an RA, students find success in organizations such as:

- Departmental Organizations and Clubs
- Intramural Teams or Clubs
- Honor Societies (Scholastic International Honor Societies and Departmental Honor Societies)
- **Sororities** and **Fraternities** (Greek Life)
- Special Interest Organizations and Clubs (Latino Student Association, National Society of Black Engineers, Gay Pride Alliance)
- Student Government Association (SGA)

I HAVE HEARD MANY INTERESTING THINGS ABOUT COLLEGE. IS IT ALL TRUE? IF SO, WHAT CAN I DO ABOUT IT?

"Youth passes, but immaturity can last a lifetime."

—Unknown

College is a great time in your life. However, college is different now. Violence, sexual assault, alcohol and drug abuse all have the potential of occurring on college campuses. In fact, every year on many college campuses, cases of violence, alcohol abuse, and sexual assault go unreported. While institutions do as much as they can to prevent these events from occurring, they cannot monitor every situation. If you make smart decisions, you greatly reduce your chances of being a victim or statistic. It is all about doing it the right way. This aspect of college life can negatively affect everything else if you approach it without careful consideration. The following tips will help you become more aware of some of the situations that you may be encounter while in college.

TIP #1: It Could Happen To You, Too. If I collected $10 for every time I have heard students say that it will never happen to them, I would be a very rich man. On a college campus, you will hear several stories about "the student who ..., or that kid, or I heard that...." Believe me you do not want to be that person. Nevertheless, every year, someone thinks that it cannot happen to them, but it does. Learn from other's mistake. You have had the opportunity to learn from other's make mistakes throughout your life. College should be no different.

TIP #2: Do Not Put Yourself Out There. Be careful what you post on your Facebook or MySpace account or any other sites that you use to communicate with friends. I have known students to put all of their information on the Website including their address, cell numbers, class schedule, and other private information. I cannot state this point enough: When you live on a college campus, you are in a public space. As much as campuses try their best to keep students safe, nothing can keep you safer than your own common sense. Therefore, be sure the information that you share is with your friends only and not with everyone else. Otherwise, you may receive unwanted attention.

> ## A QUICK WORD ABOUT ... BUT EVERYBODY IS DOING IT
>
> Contrary to popular belief, not everyone on a college campus is engaging in high-risk behaviors. If you were to examine popular culture and movies you would think that this is true. The reality is that this is not typical behavior. People usually get involved in these kinds of activities due to sheer boredom or curiosity. Some get involved in high risk behavior because it seems like everybody is doing it. College is a privilege and not a right, so be responsible for your actions.

TIP #3: Alcohol Education 101. Should you choose to drink, be aware of the consequences that come with drinking. From getting documented by a university official to being in the hospital due to an alcohol overdose, realize that it only takes one bad night for your life to be forever changed. I cannot tell you how many students have come in my office who cannot recall what happened to them on the night that they were drunk. The only thing that some of these students remember is waking up in the hospital hooked up to an I.V. If you decide to drink, know your limits. If you have never drank before and you want to see what it is like, do it with a group of people you know you can absolutely trust. Each year binge drinking contributes to student health problems, and other complications. Nationally, there have been several deaths across college campuses related to alcohol abuse.

TIP #4: No Means No. Drinking and promiscuity more often than not have a way of making situations even worse. When I was in graduate school, I knew of a male student accused of raping another student. Whether he was guilty or not, the thing that mattered most was that he was charged. As a result, the university dismissed him. His life and reputation were forever changed. This all could have been avoided if alcohol and sex were not mixed. Men need to know that it doesn't matter at what point "No" is said, women have this right at any point during sexual activity. When a person has had one two many drinks, their judgment is impaired.

TIP #5: You Wore That? This advice goes out to the ladies. In a perfect world, you would be able to wear what you wanted without anyone harassing you. However, we do not live in a perfect world. This is especially true on a college campus. When going out, understand the type of attention you may inadvertently attract with what you may be wearing. No one ever deserves to be harassed or assaulted. You may attract the attention that you want, however, it is always a stronger possibility that you will attract the wrong attention as well.

TIP #6: Damage Control. If you have been assaulted or harassed in any way, the first thing to do is to seek help. As tough as it may be, it is in your best interest to seek professional help. Whether it be a counselor, police officer, residence hall staff member, or medical staff, it is far better to address a problem immediately. I know it is hard. Its one of the toughest things you can do, but I assure you if you wait, your problems will not go away. They will only fester. There is always a healing process when you have been hurt. The healing process starts with letting someone else know about what happened to you.

TIP #7: If You Plan To Be Sexually Active, Use Protection. I know you've probably heard this time and time again. In college, we all are guilty of making poor decisions. However, one bad decision that you cannot afford to make is not using a contraceptive. A moment of pleasure can never compensate for an unplanned future. If you make the decision to engage in sexual activity, understand the consequences. Most health centers on college campuses give free contraceptives to students. If you plan to be sexually active, be sure to visit the Health Center early. They also test for HIV/AIDS and other Sexually Transmitted Diseases (STDs). You should not be ashamed to be tested. If STDs were not a reality on college campuses, these centers would not provide contraceptives or offer services. Although contraceptives do substantially reduce the risk of pregnancies and infections, the best contraceptive is abstinence.

> "Significant problems you face cannot be solved at the same level of thinking we were at when we created them."
>
> —*Albert Einstein*

TIP #8: Wait Awhile. In college, you will meet many people to whom you are attracted. If you decide to get into a relationship with that person, really get to know the person. Everyone has baggage. Many bad relationships occur because of someone not paying attention to the warning signs. Deep down inside, you know what these warning signs are. No matter how sexy, cute, or sweet they appear to be, get to know them first. I am no relationship expert, but I can promise you time always tells the story that you should hear.

TIP #9: Lock Your Doors. Institutions try their very best to promote community and safety, however, theft can happen anywhere. If you are keeping your doors unlocked—be it a vehicle or your room, you are making a big mistake. On and off campus thieves know that when students come to campus, they bring many valuable possessions. If you simply lock your door, you greatly reduce your chances of becoming a victim.

TIP #10: Get Those Digits. Knowing the emergency numbers on a college campus is very important because it could save your life or the life of a friend. Enter the school's emergency number in your cell phone or on a card that is accessible. Most schools have their own police officers and because of this, they have their own number. If you try to call 911 in an emergency, you will probably receive the dispatcher outside of the school. Thus, if you have an emergency, you will lose valuable time. If you want to know the public safety number, you can visit the school's Website or call the school's operator. Again, knowing a number could mean the difference between life and death.

TIP #11: If You Go To A Party, Stay With The Same Group. You would not believe how many bad things have happened because someone left a party alone. The possibilities range from getting lost and taking forever to get home to being robbed or assaulted. This is of great importance on any campus, especially those campuses that host parties at local clubs or off-campus. Many different type of people attend college and live near the school. Do not leave the party unless you are with someone you know very well.

TIP #12: Communicate With Each Other. Although you never think about the worst scenarios happening at a party, it is a good idea to designate a "guardian" for the night. Having a guardian is especially helpful if you are traveling as a group. The guardian is the person who can serve as the designated driver or who checks on other people. While it may be more responsibility for one person, it helps.

TIP #13: Get Tested. If you have been sexually active before college, get tested before you go to college. Being tested before you go to college gives you a better idea about where you stand. Due to the frequent sexual activity on most campuses, you can never be too safe.

TIP #14: College Can Be A Riot. In the last few decades, more sports related riots have emerged on college campuses. When I attended my graduate institution, I saw three different riots. Riots can create the type of excitement that few of us have experienced. If you do attend a campus where riots do or can take place, make sure you are not a part of them. Many students have been expelled from the campus due to participation in a riot. Some students have been seriously injured and even killed. If you plan to attend a riot, realize that things can easily get out of control.

TIP #15: Do Not Tell Your Business. This next piece of advice may come as a surprise for some and not for others. A college campus is a community. Whenever you have a community, people exchange gossip every day. If you plan to do something that you do not want everyone to know, do not tell anyone at the school. Aside risking the communication of your private life across the campus, it is best that you do not tell anyone. Although girls are notorious for gossip, guys are gossips, too!

TIP #16: Be Careful. I must put this bluntly: Date-rape drugs are frequently used on college campuses and night clubs. This is a fact. If you are planning to drink alcohol or smoke marijuana, it could be combined with another drug. Equally important, if you want to put down your drink, know that it takes just a split second for someone to slip something into your drink. If you want to avoid this, the best thing to do is to be cautious of what you eat and drink when you are at parties where you are surrounded by individuals you do not know well.

TIP #17: Safety First. Become familiar with the building exits in both academic and residential buildings. No one ever wants to experience a life-threatening emergency, but that doesn't mean that you should not plan for it. It could mean the difference between life and death.

As a child growing up in the 1980s, I remember seeing a lot of public service announcements and after school specials warning adolescents about the dangers of drugs. I remember that these announcements seemed to target high school students and not college students. Therefore, I have decided to make my own public service announcement. In college, people may try things not thinking about the immediate or long-term consequences. I wish that the words in this book could persuade you not to make costly mistakes. It just takes one time for an experiment to be life changing. Its ironic, how we spend so much time preparing for events and working hard to achieve a goal, when in one moment it can be taken away. There are some choices you personally make that can change your whole life. Why risk it? You are too important. Should you decide to experiment in any high risk behavior, ask yourself why you are doing this and who will be affected by your decision? Who is depending on you?

Learning to balance your social and academic experiences in college is very important. If you focus too much on one and not enough on the other, your college experience can be less memorable or end prematurely. You have to find the right balance.

THE FINAL WORD

Many people are under the belief that most students who enroll in colleges and universities graduate in four years. The general perception is that if a student does not finish college in four years something is wrong. However, the truth is that the national average for college completion is six years. After attending college for nine consecutive years, I realized that I could not be concerned with another student's time of completion. We are different learners, and we all have unique gifts and goals in life.

How many stories have you heard of older adults going back to college after 20 or 30 years of work? We often forget that education is a personal journey. You must focus on finding what you love and completing the degree. The truth is when you start a new job, you must be re-educated in order to learn the position and the culture of the environment. Learning is a life-long experience. It does not end when you graduate. Therefore, in most cases, the type of degree is less important than possessing the degree itself. Remember that you make the degree; the degree does not make you.

In summary, the key points to remember about college are the following: take responsibility because no one is going to do it for you; take advantage of your resources, don't be unafraid to ask for help, and learn to balance work and play. Although I cannot tell you what to do in college, I hope that the advice that I have provided will help you better understand and negotiate the complexities of college. The college experience is all about learning, whether it is in the classroom or out of the classroom. Many wonderful experiences await you after college. College is a tool to help you turn your dreams into reality. However, like most things in life, it is all about what you make of it!

APPENDIX A:
What I Was Not Told about College, My Journey

I recall once speaking with my mother who said to me that many authors have felt their message insignificant in the grand scheme of things. She followed by telling me "With all the books in the world, only one story is truly yours." She added, "People are counting on you to inspire and for you to offer your expertise." As I contemplated that very conversation, I thought for the longest time why my story was important to tell and how I would go about telling it. I then realized that I was a person who did not always know success the way I know it now. I, like many others, dared to be different, dared to dream, and dared to change my reality. If in 1997, someone told me that I would write a book about my voyage through college, I would not have believed them. Back then, I was unsure of the next day, let alone, being able to direct my own life. I certainly would not believe that I could eventually direct other students' lives. In the beginning, I was the common high school student. However, I was lucky to become the uncommon college student.

The one thing that I think about from time to time was my life before attending college. Before I take you on my journey through college, I must add some context and speak about my last year of high school. I begin my story in the spring of 1996. It was late March; the weather was sunny, warm, and pleasant. Life seemed perfect; I did not have a care in the world. I enjoyed a game of one-on-one basketball with my best friend, Gary. Gary was the other brother that I always wanted. He was smart, funny, and someone that could always make me laugh. He was also very athletic. He was quick on the dribble and had a great jump shot. Game after game we played, until eventually, we became too tired to play anymore. Consequently, we called it a draw and agreed to finish the game the next day. However, little did he or I know it would be the last time we ever played, talked, or laughed together. That day, his last words to me were "see you later," and I said the same.

On Monday, the following day, I was feeling a little under the weather so I didn't go to school. Instead, I lay in bed, since my mama advised that I get plenty of rest, and I relaxed most of the day. As hours passed, I found myself restless. Time goes by slowly when you have nothing to do. Therefore, I slept. A few hours later, I got up because my stomach was still upset. I could not find my medicine around the house, so I went to the store to get some medicine.

When I returned from the store, I saw a friend who asked me in a matter of fact manner if I knew about the fight that had taken place earlier that day. He said, "Some boy who was in ROTC at Eleanor Roosevelt High School and worked at McDonald's with you was stabbed." When I heard this, the only person that came to mind was Gary. Both my heart and mouth dropped in a state of shock. I immediately ran to Gary's apartment, which was only about two blocks away. When I arrived, no one was home. Moments later, his father pulled up. In a panic, I asked him if anything had happened to Gary. He was not aware of the fight that had happened earlier. Soon afterward, we questioned Jay, the source of my information. After gaining more details from Jay, we hurried to Prince George's County Hospital.

When we arrived, we were praying that it was not serious, but God did not answer our prayers, for Gary was dead. Gary's father and I both watched this tragedy unfold, and we found ourselves overwhelmed in a tide of tears. We viewed Gary's body one last time, but no togetherness could compensate for the helplessness and sadness that we felt.

Suddenly, without prediction or warning the wonderful spring that seemed perfect, became the frigid winter that lingered like the visit of an unwanted guest. I found myself unmistakably at the most difficult moment in my life. My best friend, with whom just the day before I spent a regular day, was gone. I would never see again the one whom I had loved like a brother.

The period from the day of the tragedy until the day of his funeral was without a doubt a trying time for many others and me as well. That week I witnessed incurable heartaches, unity in a divided community, and closeness of family and friends. In addition to this tapestry of life's melodrama, I also found hidden strength, courage, and composure within myself. During this period, I began to value friends and family more than ever. I also realized that life is not promised but rather, much like the inconsistent weather, life is here today and gone tomorrow.

SUMMER OF 1996

Despite this major traumatic experience in my life, on June 5, 1996, I crossed my high school graduation stage, becoming one of the few members in my family to receive a high school diploma. At the time, graduating high school was one of my biggest achievements. Since I had overcome so much to reach this point in my life, I thought I was ready to face the world. Earlier that year, I had decided that instead of going to college, I would enlist in the military. In high school, I was not a particularly motivated student; my grades demonstrated this fact. Aside from wanting to get away and enlist with Gary, I am not sure why I wanted to enlist in the Marine Corps. Regardless of the reason, by summer's end I would be one of the few and the proud. However, fortunately for me, I decided at the last minute not to go into the armed forces. Perhaps being hospitalized a week before being shipped off or maybe consistently running into a former disgruntled Marine changed my mind; at any rate, I decided that I did not want to enlist in the Marine Corps. Of course, this decision did not go over well with my recruiter. He was pissed off; there is no other way to explain his reaction. I remember my recruiter taking me to his office and telling me that they did not need me anyway because they had already made their numbers for that month. He also went on to say that the Marine Corps did not need pussies. After giving me an ear full, he took me home, and I never saw him again. I went on to spend the rest of the summer unemployed and even more uncertain about my future.

The autumn of 1996 brought frustration and feelings of failure. I worked at a warehouse stuffing envelopes all day. At the time, I felt like my choice not to go into the military was a huge mistake. I had to wake early each morning just to go to a job that I hated. I cannot begin to explain how much I hated that job, because I knew I was destined for something better. In retrospect, working that terrible job was one of the best things that could happen to me, because it motivated me to make something more of my life. Because it was a position for a temporary agency, work was not a guarantee. Subsequently, I was laid off and just as quickly, I became more convinced that I wanted to achieve more out of life. I do not believe that it was a question of whether I was smart enough to achieve in life but, rather, if the opportunity would ever come along.

After being laid off, I could not find another job and I was not in school. While some of my friends from high school had seemingly moved on with their lives, there I was, unemployed, frustrated and unclear of the direction I should take. My choices were severely limited. Prior to graduating from high school, my homeroom teacher advised me that maybe I should go to Prince George's Community College. Back then, this suggestion seemed a bit insulting, because I was supposedly her top student. If she was recommending community college, then how could I possibly be her top student? Besides, everyone knew community college was the 13th grade. In fact, it was across the street from another high school. As the saying goes, desperate times call for desperate measures and after assessing my own situation, suddenly community college did not seem like such a bad idea.

PRINCE GEORGE'S COMMUNITY COLLEGE

Unashamed and humbled, in the spring semester of 1997, I enrolled as a full-time student at Prince George's Community College. It only took me a couple of weeks to discover that my ideas about community college being the 13th grade were very wrong. Indeed, I found community college to be a place that cultivated growth and success. If you were willing to work hard, good things would happen. I arrived full of academic deficiencies but determined to make things work. Right before I enrolled, my family was not doing the best financially. In spite of this, my mother believed that I would succeed, so she wrote a check for $185 to cover the rest of my tuition that my financial aid package did not cover. Neither of us knew that would be the last check that she would ever need to write for me.

I had no idea that the day I set foot in community college would be the day that my life would forever change. I knew that going back to school would not be easy, but I also knew that failure was not an option. What other options did I have? Go back and work in the warehouse stuffing envelopes? The answer was clear to me: Work hard and never ever look back. As clear as this goal was to me, my first semester presented different challenges in and outside of the classroom that were very discouraging. One notable challenge was scoring below the required score on the math placement test. This of course meant that I had to take remedial math classes before I could take the required math classes that counted toward my degree. Despite this setback, some brighter days were ahead.

After my first semester at Prince George's Community College, I earned a 4.0 GPA. Consequently, the college offered me one of their most prestigious scholarships, the Apartment and Office Building Association (AOBA) scholarship. Not only did this scholarship furnish a means to pay for school, but it also provided me with an opportunity to intern in the summer for Kay Management, one of the company members within this organization. Prior to this scholarship, I had to work to cover college cost. I also had to do this while catching two long bus rides to and from school. With the scholarship, I could now completely focus on school without the distraction of work. As a result, other doors were beginning to open. This scholarship was a turning point in my early college career. The exposure that this scholarship provided me was simply the best. I still can remember sitting at tables and having conversations with politicians and multi-millionaires.

This kind of interaction has a way of changing your perspective about life. I had never envisioned myself sitting with multi-millionaires and politicians when just the year before, I was working in a poorly lit warehouse stuffing envelopes and feeling uncertain if I would have a job the next day. After being on a scholarship for two years, I felt grateful and honored to have been apart of such a tremendous experience. Although it seemed that I had arrived at a level of success, I knew that I was always a step away from waking up at 5 a.m. and finding myself working in a warehouse. So, I remained focused on my goal. As I understood it, having a college degree would allow me to have more options.

I remember being in high school and having friends that lived in middle-class neighborhoods. Seeing these homes made me think about what life had to offer in comparison to where I was living at the time. Not until I graduated from college did I begin to envision myself owning one of these homes. I realized that I was not necessarily stuck in my situation and that if I worked hard, I could achieve unbounded success.

Make no mistake, over the course of my three years at Prince George's Community College, I encountered plenty of distractions, failures, and disappointments: failing to pass a developmental math class for two consecutive semesters, seeing a friend go to jail, dealing with the drama of the near divorce of my parents, supporting my mother through a very serious surgery, and considering quitting school to work full-time. At times, it just seemed like it was too much happening at once.

Besides self-determination, I think what made me keep going was the support that I received while I was in school. I had great mentors who would not allow me to give up. They would always say to me, "I know you can't see where you are going, but we can." "Keep working hard, we know you can do it." Through all the difficulties, these special people encouraged and supported me. Before the start of my last year, I remember expressing to my mentor, Janice that I just got a new job and that it paid quite well. While she was very excited about my success, she also cautioned me not to get comfortable because she felt that I was destined for greater things. I really wanted her to be excited about my opportunity, but I realized that she saw the big picture and she wanted to see me in that big picture. Like most community college students who had a "good paying job", I fell into the trap of questioning the necessity to transfer to a four-year institution. After all, I was in the midst of finishing my associate's degree. Nevertheless, I did not let the lure of a well paying job distract me, and I continued to press forward.

During the second semester of my last year, I was not sure what I was going to do about transferring until another mentor of mine, Beth Atkins, told me about a transfer scholarship at Morgan State University. Prior to this conversation, I knew little about this school, so I did my research. As luck would have it, Morgan State had the major I was planning to declare. All I needed was a 3.5 GPA to get a full academic scholarship. At the time, I had a 3.4 GPA; thus, I was short and only had two semesters to make the grade. I was not sure how I was going to reach my goal because I had to take two math classes and a philosophy class that everyone seemed to barely pass. I never wanted something so badly, and I never worked so hard in my life. Throughout all of my schooling, math was my hardest subject. Having to take math was like having to work with the classmate you did not want to work with, but you had to in order to pass the class. Despite my failing two developmental math classes two consecutive semesters, I had to win. I remember staying up late nights reworking math problems, spending hours and hours rewriting philosophy papers, and spending weekends at the tutorial center. All the while, I was getting up 4 a.m. in the morning to be at work by 6 a.m. They say that if you want success, you have to be willing to pay the price. I was more than willing to pay the price because I knew that my success would pay the price of my schooling. I remember having to say no to my friends when it came to hanging out. Believe me, I did my share of hanging out, but I had to stay focused. There was simply too much at stake. My future depended on my academic success. At the end of the fall semester, I earned a 3.8, which brought me to a 3.49, and the following semester I earned a 4.0, which took me to a 3.52. Suffice to say, I accomplished my goal. Morgan State University awarded me a full academic scholarship!

MORGAN STATE UNIVERSITY

On May 25, 2000, I graduated from Prince George's Community College with an associate's degree. I was very proud of my accomplishments, but I was not done yet. Unlike before, I now felt certain of my future and good about the direction that I was heading. More focused than ever, I was fully prepared to transfer to Morgan State University. Although my leaving home ultimately affected some of my relationships, I knew I was doing the right thing. If these relationships were truly meant to last, they would last. Morgan State University, located in Baltimore, seemed like the best choice for me. It was close enough to home but far enough from distractions. My first year at Morgan was an absolute success: Not only did I earn a 3.8 GPA, but I also became very involved in campus life. So much so, that the following year I became President of the Society of Future Educators, a Resident Assistant, and an inductee in the Golden Key International Honor Society.

My success during my first year was largely due to the help of many people supporting and believing in me, namely Dr. Wright, my academic advisor and mentor. She was definitely someone who made me feel like I could do anything. One of the skills that I had mastered at Prince George's Community College was networking and seeking out resources. Mr. Gwynn, who was at the time my Resident Director, in many ways was the man responsible for pushing me toward the field of higher education. A classy gentleman, he definitely saw something in me that I did not see in myself at the time. However, I guess that's how college works: You meet people that help you see your potential and then they help you reach your goal.

At Morgan, success continued to roll in like tidal waves. During the 2002–2003 academic year, I was appointed by the governor of Maryland to serve as Student Commissioner for the Maryland Higher Education Commission (MHEC). MHEC was the coordinating organization for all postsecondary institutions in the state of Maryland. The organization gives recommendations to the governor of Maryland, who forwards these recommendations to the state legislature to appropriate money. The Student Commissioner position was the most coveted position in the state because they represented the interests and needs of all higher education students in the state of Maryland. If anyone epitomized the college student, it was I. I was familiar with living on campus and being a student leader. I was familiar with commuting to and form campus while working full time, and I knew what it was like to come to school having academic deficiencies to bridge. Obtaining this position was arguably one of the most distinguished triumphs of my college career. Being appointed Student Commissioner was very significant because just five years earlier, I was at one of the lowest points of my life. Suddenly, I was standing tall at the summit of my college career.

This position taught me a great deal about the business, the politics, and the conversations that take place behind the scenes in higher education. I felt both grateful and privileged to serve in this position. My taking this position came on the heels of one of MHECs most conversational years in which students were protesting the increase of tuition in many of Maryland's colleges and they demanded that MHEC stand behind their requests. In addition to the protests that same year, MHEC entered into an agreement with the Office of Civil Rights to agree to recommend increased funding for Historically Black

Colleges and Universities (HBCUs) in the state of Maryland. Consequently, I was not stepping into an easy role.

On the flip side to all of the success that I was experiencing, I found out that with achievement comes isolation and loneliness. During that year, I found out that plaques, medals, and certificates do not always provide fulfillment. I had everything that most students wanted: good grades, accolades, and a promising future. Amidst all of the success, there was something missing. I felt disconnected from my family and friends on and off campus. I never once took the time to consider the other side of success. Although, I should have been happy, I struggled socially. In retrospect, there were plenty of opportunities for hooking up but I wanted someone to spend my time with when I was not playing college administrator. I wanted to share my success with someone. I would be remiss if I did not mention that I did meet girls on and off campus, though there was only one that I found myself crazy about. We were on and off for two straight years.

Back then, I could give you all of the reasons why I wanted her, but I could not give you any reasons why it never worked. I remember all of the crazy stuff that I did for her. I remember being at her track meet all day on my birthday, and her not even remembering my birthday. I remember driving fourteen hours in one day just to take her to meet her lifelong hero, Carl Brashear. I remember being in the hospital with her from 9 p.m. to 4 a.m. only to find out that she was pregnant by another guy. Looking back, I saw all of the signs, yet I still tried to make it work. After many disappointments, I finally decided that I did not need the drama, so I moved on.

Although I wanted things to work out badly, I finally realized that she was not the one for me. In life, you know some people are not right for you, but you try to make it work anyway. We all learn from these situations; I know I did. Although I eventually moved on, I do not regret anything that happened. I am just glad I was able to stay focused. The social aspect of college was something that my advisor never told me about when I was in high school. Life is unpredictable and college is no different.

SUMMER OF 2003—GOVENOR'S INTERNSHIP

The summer of 2003 was an interesting summer. I was one of nineteen Maryland students selected as part of the Governor's Summer Internship Program, which provided an opportunity for college students to gain first-hand experience working in top-level state government agencies. Specifically, I interned within the Division of Corrections for the Department of Public Safety. This was a good experience because I had an opportunity to understand how this particular department functioned. I also got an opportunity to work on a policy paper that we presented to the governor of Maryland at the conclusion of the program. On the other hand, working in this division was depressing.

In visiting correction facilities, the overwhelming majority of the prisoners that I saw were young black men between the ages of 16 and 40. I think what was so heartbreaking for me was that I knew all of the potential that society was losing. I just knew that there were great leaders, entrepreneurs, engineers, fathers, and husbands in those prisons, but somehow they made the wrong decisions. Each time after visiting one of the facilities, I thought about the differences that separated us. Specifically, what experiences could have changed either of our circumstances where they would have ended up visiting me? I also thought about why I was chosen to see this. I never could figure out the answer, but one thing was certain—I felt an even greater obligation to succeed. While I had achieved a level of success, I knew that it came with much responsibility.

During one particular visit, as an officer escorted me throughout the facility and told me about the inmate population, an old friend recognized me. The officer told me that one of the inmates wanted to speak with me. Of course my first reaction was who and why. Reluctantly, I went back into the facility, and there was Fred. Fred was one of my childhood friends that I grew up with in Landover, MD. At the age of 16, he started selling drugs, and eventually found himself in and out of the Maryland prison system. I believe in my heart that Fred was a good person, but for one reason or another, he could not resist the lure of fast money, peer pressure, and materialism. While our conversation was not long, I gave him my address, and we kept in touch. In a letter, I discovered that Fred was not the only person from my old neighborhood who had been in and out of prison. After seeing Fred, I realized just how much divine intervention, hard work, and the support of others had to do with the many blessings in my life. As much as I had accomplished, I never felt like I was too far removed from Fred's situation.

FINAL YEAR—2003–2004

The 2003–2004 school year, brought challenges, victories, and opportunities. First, I finally slayed the dragon called the Praxis. The Praxis is the teacher's certification test. I had to take this test four times before receiving the composite score that I needed to be admitted into student teaching, the last phase of my degree program. Without question, persistence was the key. In addition, I was elected Vice-President of the Student Government Association (SGA). Despite all the responsibility, my hard work finally paid off, and I was looking squarely at the finish line. It was perhaps one of my best years at Morgan State, and yet, some of the toughest months of my life.

Being SGA Vice President gave me a great opportunity to serve my fellow students; however, I did not expect what was ahead. During our one-year tenure, three students were killed off campus between the time we were inaugurated and the end of our term. Indeed, these were tough times for the students and administration. Having already experienced a similar situation, it feel like deja vu. I remember saying to myself, "this is not supposed to happen in college." Despite the number of times you lose students, you never know what to do or say. As an administration, we went in with intentions of making things right. One year prior to taking office, SGA saw many tough days: an SGA member being accused of sexual harassment and the SGA President Elect being impeached due to poor grades.

At the very beginning of our tenure, according to students and administrators, we were viewed as the SGA administration that would bring back the glory days. We were serious about service, but by the end of our term, we were more than willing to pass the torch. I was definitely burning out. When the spring semester arrived, my burnout became even more evident. During the spring semester, I was student teaching and maintaining many of my other responsibilities. My weekdays started at 5:45 a.m. and did not usually end until after midnight. I had no time for me, let alone for the students I served. As the semester progressed, I became more and more stressed. I remember one day collapsing on my bed from exhaustion and not waking up until the next morning.

Many students were excited about finally having the opportunity to put their knowledge to practical use, but I was no longer passionate about being a teacher. My passion had become higher education, and I felt like I was in a marriage where I wanted a divorce. Subsequently, this experience was one of the hardest experiences that I had ever endured because I was tapped out physically and mentally on a daily basis.

One of the sad truths that I discovered first hand from this experience was that many teachers had little parental support and scarce resources. Being a teacher is one of the most admirable and important positions that anyone could have, and yet it is the most unappreciated and unsupported. I discovered that unless you were in a good community, teachers did not have the support or resources they needed to fulfill their jobs. I also discovered that the policy No Child Left Behind really should have been called All The Poor Children Left Behind. If America's educational systems are to improve, serious reform must start with our public school systems. When I was student teaching, I had the opportunity to work in two very different school systems (Baltimore City and Howard County). As it came to no surprise, third graders in the suburbs knew their timetables much better than fifth graders in the inner city. Baltimore City students seem to be set up for failure and disappointment from the start. Although the students that I worked with in Baltimore City had great teachers, they did not have adequate resources. I think I could have been a great asset to the school system, but my heart was not in it. Like everyone else, I just wanted to be passionate about what I was doing. Toward the end, I remember many nights only getting a few hours of sleep. As the saying goes, what does not kill you only makes you stronger. What got me through was the support I received from my friends, family, and mentors.

Long before my student teaching experience and even more so afterward, I knew that working in some aspect of higher education was what I wanted to do with my career. I can truly say that no student on campus was as privileged enough to view higher education from as many perspectives as I did. A great part of my personal development has come from being involved in school. Although I did not get involved as a student leader within a student organization at community college, I took advantage of every opportunity that came my way. My undergraduate experience was not typical, but I believe that I benefited the most because of the three years I spent at Prince George's Community College. Lessons learned there made me more mature and academically ready for Morgan State University.

UNIVERSITY OF MASSACHUSETTS AMHERST

After graduating from Morgan State University, I enrolled into the master's program of higher education administration at the University of Massachusetts Amherst (UMASS). I was excited, poised, and ready to take on any challenge that was in front of me. Amherst, Massachusetts, was very different from Baltimore, MD. Amherst was truly an adjustment for me, because not only did people seem very unfriendly but also the winters were really, really cold. I also had to learn how to negotiate an environment with a very different population of people.

Prior to graduate school, I had never been in a rural area or an area that was heavily populated by Caucasians. Just when you think you have something mastered, life always has a way of presenting you with different challenges. The one difficulty that I faced for the first time was the absence of the social support system that I had at the last two institutions. This part of my journey was by far the most challenging because I was in an environment in which I didn't always feel comfortable. It was an entirely different world. Initially, I did not know anyone and for the first time in college, I was a part of the minority population. At Morgan State, I never tried to fit in; I just fit. Even though we all had different experiences, we could relate to each other without much effort. I felt no pressure to prove how smart or competent I was in school. I never had to answer questions about my experiences, black culture, or even my hair. I never had to be the Black culture teacher to other people. In my opinion, this feeling of self-assurance had a lot to do with being in an environment where you felt comfortable and nurtured. Although I did eventually find social support at UMASS, it was unlike any other experience in college.

One defining moment that took place during my first winter break of graduate school involved a friend from back home. While I was home for winter break, my friend, Lloyd, whom I had not seen since graduation picked me up so that we could get something to eat. Unbeknownst to me until he pointed it out, he had in the car with him a handgun and a bag of marijuana. After he showed me this, I asked him why he was doing this, and why did he pick me up. He tried to explain, but nothing he said could make me understand his rationale. At that moment, it seemed that my whole life flashed in front of me, and I had to make a decision about what I was going to do. I just knew if we continued on our journey somehow, we would be pulled over by the police. I had been harassed by the police before when I did nothing wrong, so I had an idea how this incident could potentially end. The life that I had worked so hard to establish would be gone in an instant. Without any hesitation, I told him to take me back home.

From that point on, I knew that I needed to be careful about individuals with whom I associated myself with from my old neighborhood. I think one of the hardest things to do when you go to college is to say goodbye to old friends. Lloyd and I had been friends for about six years, yet I had to end our friendship for the sake of my future. Looking back, I have no regrets, because I know that we were at two different points in our lives. I had a responsibility not only to myself, but also to all who saw me as a role model. Although I never had to end a friendship quite like this before, I had no problem with cutting ties. In many ways, this incident was symbolic of my complete transition that began seven years earlier.

After returning to school from winter break, I made more of an effort to form relationships. I became grateful for those relationships and grateful for where I was in life. Although my major was higher education administration, I received a heavy dose of social justice literature in most of my courses. Through many of the readings, I learned how inequalities are replicated systemically. I learned that racism, sexism, and the other various "isms" were alive and well.

Above all, however, I learned that nothing could stop me but me. I think this rule applies to anyone. If you want something badly, you can get it!

Throughout my college experience, I had demonstrated this consistently. My graduate school experience should have been no different. However, self-doubt always reintroduced itself back into my life. No matter how many mountains I had climbed before, there was always another. I remember many late nights working on papers and thinking to myself, "Why am I here?" "I have a college degree, so I can go back home and work." "I have already beaten the odds." In the past, it seemed that every time I started to talk this way, my mentors would show up like superheroes and say otherwise. Luckily, for me, this proved to be the case.

My mentor at UMASS was Dr. Shederick McClendon, a professor in the higher education program. Dr. McClendon was a strong black man who had very high standards, and he expected nothing but excellence from anything or anyone with where he had an affiliation. Dr. McClendon never allowed me to settle for mediocrity. He took a vested interest in me, because someone did it for him. He was another mentor who cared enough to keep motivating me when I felt like quitting. I remember many of our conversations, in which he always pushed me to do more. If I got a B, he would say that I could do better. No matter the task, he always got me to dig deeper. We all need mentors like that in our lives, because they inspire us to go beyond our comfort zone and believe in ourselves.

They also help us stay focused. Although, I was self-motivated, I am not sure if I would have finished graduate school without him, because he made me feel like I belonged. Although I never did get completely comfortable at UMASS, I did grow as a whole person. I had my share of struggles but it was a necessary and good experience. An important lesson that I learned at UMASS was that change is a part of life. With change, you must learn to adapt and accept what you have no control over. With that said, I learned to be vulnerable. After opening myself to new friendships and experiences, I was able to grow as both a student and person. Once again, what got me through the difficult moments was the support of friends, mentors, and colleagues who were willing to help me because I was willing to accept help. While this is a reoccurring mantra in my college experience, I believe that everyone should adopt this same philosophy: You cannot get through college without the support of others. The college experience is not designed that way.

After two years of working hard, I graduated with my master's degree in Higher Education Administration. After a tedious job search process that took me from the east coast to the west coast, I eventually got a job at the University of Dayton. Today, I work as a campus administrator helping students through their complex college journey, much like others did for me during my college years.

APPENDIX B:
Useful Websites

Here are some websites and books that are helpful in your postsecondary education journey.

Accreditation:

http://www.chea.org/search/default.asp
Council for Higher Education Accreditation (CHEA) database

Athletic Scholarships:

www.edref.com/athletic-scholarships
www.ncaa.org/about/scholarships.html

Campus Safety:

www.collegesafe.com

Career Services Support Websites:

http://www.collegegrad.com
http://www.interbiznet.com/hunt/
www.monster.com

College Research and Homework Websites:

http://www.algebra-online.com   Algebra Online
http://www.encyberpedia.com/ency.htm   Encyberpedia
www.bjpinchbeck.com   Homework Helper

http://www.libraryspot.com	Library Spot
http://www.loc.gov	Library of Congress
http://www.refdesk.com/main.html	My Virtual Reference Desk
http://www.s9.com/biography	Noble Citizens of Planet Earth
http://www.onelook.com	One Look Dictionaries
www.dictionary.com	Online Dictionary
http://owl.english.purdue.edu	Online Writing Lab-Purdue University
http://www.sci.lib.uci.edu/~martindale/Ref.html	Reference Desk
http://www.ipl.org/ref	Reference Center
http://www.researchpaper.com/directory.html	Researchpaper.com
http://www.studyweb.com	Study Web
http://thorplus.lib.purdue.edu/reference/index.html	The Virtual Reference Desk

College Search Information

American Council on Education
http://www.collegeispossible.org
American Indian Higher Education Consortium
http://www.aihec.org/
Community College Directory
http://www.community-college.org/
Council for Christian Colleges and Universities
http://www.cccu.org/about/members.asp
Directory of Private Colleges and Universities
http://www.privatecolleges.com
Hispanic Association of Colleges and Universities Directory
http://www.hacu.net/hacu/
Historically Black College and University Directory
http://www.ed.gov/about/inits/list/whhbcu/edlite-list.html
Index of American Universities
http://www.clas.ufl.edu/au/
The World's Most Complete Education-Index
www.braintrack.com
Virtual Campus Tours
http://www.campustours.com

Financial Aid Information:

http://www.college-scholarships.com
http://www.collegeboundfund.com
http://www.edfund.org
htpp://www.educaid.com
http://www.fafsa.ed.gov
http://www.finaid.org
http://www.freegovmoney.net
http://www.nela.net
http://www.salliemae.com

General Scholarship Information

http://www.fastweb.com
http://www.freescholarshipsearch.com
http://scholarshipcoach.com
http://www.scholarshipexpert.com
http://www.scholarships.com
http://www.srnexpress.com

Health Information

http://www.nalusda.gov/fnic	Food and Nutrition Information
http://www.menshealth.com	Men's Health Daily
http://www.shapeup.org/sua	Shape Up America
http://www.womens-health.com	Women's Health Interactive

Learning Styles and Learning Disabilities

http://www.chadd.org	Children and Adults with Attention Deficit Disorder
http://www.keirsey.com	Keirsey Web Site

New/Used College Textbooks Online

www.abebooks.com
www.bigwords.com
www.bookfinder.com
www.bookmooch.com
www.cheapestbookprice.com
www.efollett.com

www.textbook411.com
www.textbooks.com
www.thriftbooks.com
www.valorebooks.com
www.varsitybooks.com

Resident Assistant and Higher Education Career Information

www.Academic360.com
http://www.acuho.ohio-state.edu/
www.HigherEdJobs.com
www.residentassistant.com
www.resnet.com
www.studentaffairs.com

SAT and ACT Information

| www.act.org | ACT Information |
| www.collegeboard.com | SAT and ACT Information |

Study Abroad Information

http://www.iie.org//programs/gilman/index.html	Benjamin A. Gillman Scholarship
http://www.iie.org/pgms	Institute of International Education
http://www.iefa.org	International Education Financial Aid
http://www.internationalscholarships.com	International Scholarships Online
http://www.thescholarship.com	The Scholar Ship
http://www.semesteratsea.com	Semester at Sea
http://www.studyabroad.com	StudyAroad.com

State Postsecondary Information

For information about state financial aid and colleges and universities in specific states, contact the organizations listed below. They can provide you with other contacts in the state for more information.

ALABAMA

Director of Grants and Scholarships
Alabama Commission on Higher Education
P.O. Box 30200
Montgomery, Alabama 36130-2000
(334) 242-2271
FAX: 242-0270
www.ache.state.al.us

ALASKA

Executive Director
Alaska Commission on Postsecondary Education
3030 Vintage Boulevard
Juneau, AK 99801-7109
(800) 441-2962
(907) 465-2962
FAX: 465-5316
www.state.ak.us/acpe

President
University of Alaska System
202 Butrovich Building
P.O. Box 755000
Fairbanks, AK 99775-5000
(907) 474-7311
FAX: 474-7570
info.alaska.edu

ARIZONA

Executive Director
Arizona Commission for Post Secondary Education
2020 North Central Ave., Suite 275
Phoenix, AZ 85004
(602) 229-2591
FAX: 229-2599
www.acpe.asu.edu

ARKANSAS

Director
Department of Higher Education
114 East Capitol
Little Rock, AR 72201
(501) 371-2000
FAX: 371-2001
www.adhe.arknet.edu

CALIFORNIA

Executive Director
California Postsecondary Education Commission
1303 J Street, Suite 500
Sacramento, CA 95814-2938
(916) 445-7933
FAX: 327-4417
www.cpec.ca.gov

California Student Aid Commission
P.O. Box 419026
Ranchero Cordova, CA 95741
(888) 224-7268
(916) 526-7590
FAX: 526-8002
www.csac.ca.gov

COLORADO

Executive Director
Colorado Commission on Higher Education
1300 Broadway, 2nd Floor
Denver, CO 80203
(303) 866-2723
FAX: 860-9750
www.state.co.us/cche_dir/hecche.html

CONNECTICUT

Commissioner of Higher Education
Department of Higher Education
61 Woodland Street
Hartford, CT 06105
(860) 947-1801
FAX: 947-1310
www.ctdhe.org

DELAWARE

Executive Director
Delaware Higher Education Commission
820 North French Street, 5th Floor
Wilmington, DE 19801
(302) 577-3240
FAX: 577-6765
www.doe.state.de.us/high-ed

DISTRICT OF COLUMBIA

Chief
Office of Postsecondary Education Research and Assistance
2100 M. L. King Jr. Avenue, S.E. #401
Washington, DC 20020
(202) 727-3685
FAX: 727-2739
www.dhs.dc.gov/info/postsecondary.shtm

FLORIDA

Executive Director
Postsecondary Education Planning Commission
Turlington Building
224 Collins Building
Tallahassee, FL 32399-0400
(850) 488-7894
FAX: 922-5388
www.cepri.state.fl.us

Office of Student Financial Assistance
255 Collins Building
325 W. Gaives Street
Tallahassee, FL 32399-0400
(850) 488-4095
FAX: 488-3612
www.firn.edu/doe

GEORGIA

Chancellor
Board of Regents
University System of Georgia
270 Washington Street, S.W.
Atlanta, GA 30334
(404) 656-2202
FAX: 657-6979
www.usg.edu

Georgia Student Finance Commission
2082 East Exchange Place
Tucker, GA 30084
(770) 414-3200
FAX: 724-9225
www.gsfc.org

HAWAII

President
University of Hawaii System
2444 Dole Street
Bachman Hall, Room 202
Honolulu, HI 96822
(808) 956-8207
FAX: 956-5286
www.hawaii.edu

Hawaii State Postsecondary Education Commission
2444 Dole Street
Bachman Hall, Room 209
Honolulu, HI 96822
(808) 956-8213
FAX: 956-5156

IDAHO

Executive Director for Higher Education
State Board of Education
P.O. Box 83720
Boise, ID 83720-0037
(208) 334-2270
FAX: 334-2632
www.sde.state.id.us/osbe/board.htm

ILLINOIS

Executive Director
Board of Higher Education
4 West Old Capitol Plaza, Room 500
Springfield, IL 62701
(217) 782-2551
FAX: 782-8548
www.ibhe.state.il.us

Illinois Student Assistance Commission
Executive Offices

500 West Monroe Street, Third Floor
Springfield, IL 62704
(217) 782-6767
FAX: 524-1858
www.isac1.org

INDIANA

Commissioner for Higher Education
Commission for Higher Education
101 West Ohio Street, Suite 550
Indianapolis, IN 46204-1971
(317) 464-4400
FAX: 464-4410
www.che.state.in.us

State Student Assistance Commission of Indiana
150 West Market Street, Suite 500
Indianapolis, IN 46204
(317) 232-2350
FAX: 232-3260
www.state.in.us/ssaci

IOWA

Executive Director
State Board of Regents, State of Iowa
100 Court Avenue, Suite 203
Des Moines, IA 50319
(515) 281-3934
FAX: 281-6420
www.state.ia.us/educate/regents

Iowa College Student Aid Commission
200 Tenth Street, 4th Floor
Des Moines, IA 50309
(515) 281-3501
FAX: 242-5996
www.state.ia.us/collegeaid

KANSAS

Executive Director
Kansas Board of Regents
700 SW Harrison, Suite 1410
Topeka, KS 66603-3760
(785) 296-3421
FAX: 296-0983
www.kansasregents.org

KENTUCKY

Executive Director
Council on Postsecondary Education
1024 Capitol Center Drive, Suite 320
Frankfort, KY 40601-8204
(502) 573-1555
FAX: 573-1535
www.cpe.state.ky.us

Kentucky Higher Education Assistance Authority
1050 U.S. 127 South
Frankfort, KY 40601
(502) 696-7200
FAX: 696-7496
www.kheaa.com

LOUISIANA

Commissioner
Board of Regents
150 Third Street, Suite 129
Baton Rouge, LA 70801-1389
(225) 342-4253
FAX: 342-9318
www.regents.state.la.us

Office of Student Financial Assistance,
Louisiana Student Financial Assistance Commission
P.O. Box 91202

Baton Rouge, LA 70821-9202
(225) 922-1011
FAX: 922-1089
www.osfa.state.la.us

MAINE

Chancellor
University of Maine System
107 Maine Avenue
Bangor, ME 04401-4380
(207) 973-3205
FAX: 973-3296
www.maine.edu

Financial Authority of Maine,
Maine Education Assistance Division
One Weston Court
State House, Station 119
Augusta, ME 04333
(800) 228-3734
(207) 626-8200
FAX: 628-8208
www.famemaine.com

MARYLAND

Secretary of Higher Education
Maryland Higher Education Commission
Jeffrey Building
16 Francis Street
Annapolis, MD 21401-1781
(410) 974-2971
FAX: 974-3513
www.mhec.state.md.us

MASSACHUSETTS

Chancellor
Massachusetts Board of Higher Education

1 Ashburton Place, Room 1401
Boston, MA 02108-1696
(617) 727-7785
FAX: 727-6397 or 727-0955
www.mass.edu

Office of Student Financial Assistance
330 Stuart Street
Boston, MA 02116
(617) 727-9420
FAX: 727-0667
www.osfa.mass.edu

MICHIGAN

Michigan Higher Education Student Loan Authority
State Department of Treasury
P.O. Box 30051
Lansing, MI 48909
(888) 643-7521
(517) 373-3662
FAX: 335-6699

Office of Scholarships and Grants
P.O. Box 30462
Lansing, MI 48909
(888) 447-2687
(517) 373-3394
FAX: 335-5984

MINNESOTA

Executive Director
Higher Education Services Office
1450 Energy Park Drive
Suite 350
St. Paul, MN 55108
(651) 642-0533
FAX: 642-0675
www.mheso.state.mn.us

MISSISSIPPI

Commissioner
Board of Trustees of State Institutions of Higher Learning
3825 Ridgewood Road
Jackson, MS 39211-6453
(601) 982-6623
FAX: 987-4172
www.ihl.state.ms.us

MISSOURI

Commissioner of Higher Education
Coordinating Board for Higher Education
3515 Amazonas Drive
Jefferson City, MO 65109-5717
(573) 751-2361
FAX: 751-6635
www.mocbhe.gov

MONTANA

Commissioner of Higher Education
Montana University System
P.O. Box 203101
Helena, MT 59620-3101
(406) 444-6570
FAX: 444-1469

NEBRASKA

Executive Director
Coordinating Commission for Postsecondary Education
P.O. Box 95005
Lincoln, NE 68509-5005
(402) 471-2847
FAX: 471-2886
http://www.ccpe.state.ne.us/PublicDoc/CCPE/default.asp

NEVADA

Chancellor
University of Nevada System
2601 Enterprise Road
Reno, NV 89512
(775) 784-4901
FAX: 784-1127
www.nevada.edu

Nevada Department of Education
700 East 5th Street
Carson City, NV 89701
(775) 687-9200
FAX: 687-9101
www.nde.state.nv.us/

NEW HAMPSHIRE

Executive Director
New Hampshire Postsecondary Education Commission
Two Industrial Park Drive
Concord, NH 03301-8512
(603) 271-2555 or 271-2695
FAX: 271-2696
www.state.nh.us/postsecondary

Chancellor
University System of New Hampshire
Dunlap Center, 25 Concord Road
Durham, NH 03824-3545
(603) 868-1800
FAX: 868-3021
www.usnh.unh.edu

NEW JERSEY

New Jersey Department of Higher Education
Office of Student Assistance and Information Systems
P.O. Box 540

Trenton, NJ 08625
1-800-792-8670
FAX: (609) 588-7285
www.hesaa.org

NEW MEXICO

Executive Director
Commission on Higher Education
1068 Cerrillos Road
Santa Fe, NM 87501-4295
(505) 827-7383
FAX: 827-7392
www.nmche.orgu

NEW YORK

Deputy Commissioner for Higher and Professional Education
Room 979EBA
New York State Education Department
Albany, NY 12234
(518) 474-5851
FAX: 486-2175
www.highered.nysed.gov

The New York State Higher Education Services Corporation
99 Washington Avenue
Albany, NY 12255
(888) 697-4372
(518) 473-0431
FAX: 473-3749
www.hesc.com

NORTH CAROLINA

Vice President for Planning
University of North Carolina
General Administration
P.O. Box 2688
Chapel Hill, NC 27515-2688

(919) 962-6981
FAX: 962-3591
www.ga.unc.edu

North Carolina State Education Assistance Authority (NCSEAA)
P.O. Box 14103
Research Triangle Park, NC 27709
(919) 549-8614
FAX: 549-8481
www.ncseaa.edu

College Foundation, Inc.
P.O. Box 12100
Raleigh, NC 27605
(888) 234-6400 (students and parents)
(800) 532-2832 (high schools and colleges)
(919) 821-4771
FAX: 821-3139
www.cfnc.org

NORTH DAKOTA

Chancellor
North Dakota University System
600 East Boulevard Avenue
Bismarck, ND 58505
(701) 328-2960
FAX: 328-2961
www.ndus.nodak.edu

OHIO

Chancellor
Ohio Board of Regents
30 East Broad Street, 36th Floor
Columbus, OH 43266-0417
(614) 466-0887
FAX: 466-5866
www.regents.state.oh.us

OKLAHOMA

Chancellor
State Regents for Higher Education
500 Education Building
State Capitol Complex
Oklahoma City, OK 73105
(405) 524-9100
FAX: 524-9230
www.okhighered.org

OREGON

Chancellor
Oregon University System
P.O. Box 3175
Eugene, OR 97403-1075
(541) 346-5700
FAX: 346-5764
www.ous.edu

Oregon State Scholarship Commission
1500 Valley River Drive, Suite 100
Eugene, OR 97401
(541) 687-7400
FAX: 687-7419
www.ossc.state.or.us

PENNSYLVANIA

Commissioner for Higher Education
State Department of Education
333 Market Street, 12th Floor
Harrisburg, PA 17126-0333
(717) 787-5041
FAX: 783-0583
www.state.pa.us

Pennsylvania Higher Education Assistance Agency
1200 North 7th Street

Harrisburg, PA 17102
(800) 692-7392 (loans)
(800) 692-7435 (grants)
(717) 257-2850
(717) 720-3644 (loans fax)
FAX: 720-3907
www.pheaa.org

PUERTO RICO

Executive Director
Council on Higher Education
P.O. Box 1900
San Juan, PR 00910-1900
(809) 724-7100
FAX: 725-1275

RHODE ISLAND

Commissioner of Higher Education
Office of Higher Education
301 Promenade Street
Providence, RI 02908-5720
(401) 222-6560
FAX: 222-6111
www.ribghe.org

Rhode Island Board of Governors
301 Promenade Street
Providence, RI 02908-5748
(401) 222-2088
FAX: 222-2545
www.ribghe.org

Rhode Island Higher Education Assistance Authority
560 Jefferson Boulevard
Warwick, RI 02886
(401) 736-1100
FAX: 732-3541
www.riheaa.org

SOUTH CAROLINA

Commissioner
Commission on Higher Education
1333 Main Street, Suite 200
Columbia, SC 29201
(803) 737-2260
FAX: 737-2297
www.che400.state.sc.us

South Carolina Higher Education Tuition Grants Commission
P.O. Box 12159
Columbia, SC 29211
(803) 734-1200
FAX: 734-1426
www.sctuitiongrants.com/

SOUTH DAKOTA

Executive Director
Board of Regents
207 East Capitol Avenue
Pierre, SD 57501-3159
(605) 773-3455
FAX: 773-5320
www.ris.sdbor.edu

Department of Education and Cultural Affairs,
Office of the Secretary
700 Governors Drive
Pierre, SD 57501-2291
(605) 773-3134
FAX: 773-6139
www.state.sd.us/deca

TENNESSEE

Executive Director
Tennessee Higher Education Commission
Parkway Towers, Suite 1900

404 James Robertson Parkway
Nashville, TN 37243-0830
(615) 741-7562
FAX: 741-6230
www.state.tn.us/thec

Tennessee Student Assistance Corporation
Parkway Towers, Suite 1950
404 James Robertson Parkway
Nashville, TN 37243-0820
800-257-6526
(615) 741-1346
FAX: 741-6101
www.state.tn.us/tsac

TEXAS

Commissioner
Texas Higher Education Coordinating Board
P.O. Box 12788
Austin, TX 78711
(512) 483-6101
FAX: 483-6169
www.thecb.state.tx.us

Texas Higher Education Coordinating Board
P.O. Box 12788
Austin, TX 78711
(512) 483-6100
FAX: 483-6169

UTAH

Commissioner of Higher Education
Utah System of Higher Education
3 Triad Center, Suite 550
Salt Lake City, UT 84180-1205
(801) 321-7101
FAX: 321-7199
www.utahsbr.edu

VERMONT

Vermont Student Assistance Corporation
P.O. Box 2000, Champlain Mill
Winooski, VT 05404-2601
(800) 642-3177
(802) 655-9602
FAX: 654-3765
www.vsac.org

Chancellor
Vermont State Colleges
P.O. Box 359
Waterbury, VT 05676
(800) 872-2205
(802) 241-2520
FAX: 241-3369
www.vsc.edu

President
University of Vermont
349 Waterman Building
Burlington, VT 05405
(802) 656-3186
FAX: 656-1363
www.uvm.edu

VIRGINIA

Director
State Council of Higher Education
101 North 14th Street, 9th Floor
Richmond, VA 23219
(804) 225-2600
FAX: 225-2604
www.schev.edu

WASHINGTON

Executive Director
Higher Education Coordinating Board
917 Lakeridge Way, P.O. Box 43430
Olympia, WA 98504-3430
(360) 753-7800
FAX: 753-7808
www.hecb.wa.gov

WEST VIRGINIA

Chancellor
State College System of West Virginia
1018 Kanawha Boulevard, East
Charleston, WV 25301
(304) 558-0699
FAX: 558-1011
www.scs.wvnet.edu

Chancellor
University System of West Virginia
1018 Kanawha Boulevard, East, Suite 700
Charleston, WV 25301
(304) 558-2736
FAX: 558-3264
www.usys.wvnet.edu

WISCONSIN

Higher Educational Aids Board
P.O. Box 7885
Madison, WI 53707
(608) 267-2206
FAX: 267-2808
heab.state.wi.us

President
University of Wisconsin System
1700 Van Hise Hall

1220 Linden Drive
Madison, WI 53706
(800) 442-6461
(608) 262-2321
FAX: 262-3985
www.uwsa.edu

WYOMING

The Community College Commission
2020 Carey Avenue, 8th Floor
Cheyenne, WY 82002
(307) 777-7763
FAX: 777-6567
www.commission.wcc.edu

President
University of Wyoming
Box 3434
Laramie, WY 82071-3434
(307) 766-4121
FAX: 766-2271 or 766-4126
www.uwyo.edu

APPENDIX C:
Recommended Readings

A Hope in the Unseen by Ron Suskind

First in the Family: Your High School Years: Advice about College from First-Generation Students by Kathleen Cushman

First in the Family: Your College Years: Advice about College from First Generation Students by Kathleen Cushman

First-Generation Students: Confronting the Cultural Issues (New Directions for Community Colleges) by L. Steven Zwerling

Live Your Dreams by Les Brown

How to Win at College: Surprising Secrets for Success from the Country's Top Students by Cal Newort

Millennials Rising: The Next Great Generation by Neil Howe and William Strauss

Been There, Should've Done That II: More Tips for Making the Most of College by Suzette Taylor

How to Go to College Almost for Free by Ben Kaplan

The College Board Scholarship Handbook 2007: All-new 10th Edition (College Board Scholarship Handbook)

Scholarships, Grants and Prizes 2007 (Peterson's Scholarships, Grants & Prizes) by Peterson's

The Money Book for the Young Fabulous & Broke by Suze Orman

GLOSSARY

Academic Advising: Assistance to students in choosing courses by providing information about majors, various academic programs, and academic policies and procedures.

Academic Advisor: A faculty or professional staff member trained to help students with selecting classes, scheduling, and choosing a major and/or minor. Advisors may also assist students in establishing their educational and career goals.

Academic Dismissal: Dismissal from a college or program for not maintaining the required grade point average (GPA). Dismissal indicates that a student is no longer a member of the institution's community.

Academic Standing: A student's academic standing is determined by the number of credit hours attempted and the number of quality points earned. There are typically five categories of academic standing: good standing, academic warning, academic probation, academic suspension, and academic dismissal. If you are on some form of financial aid, it is affected by your academic standing.

Academic Warning: The status assigned to a student with a cumulative GPA of less than 2.0.

Accelerated Study: A program of study completed in less time than is usually required, most often by attending classes in summer or by taking extra courses during the regular academic terms.

ACT: A standardized achievement examination for college admissions in the United States. The ACT measures high school students' general educational development and their ability to complete college-level work with the multiple-choice tests covering four skill areas: English, mathematics, reading, and science.

Adjunct Faculty: Part-time certified instructors.

Admission: Acceptance of an applicant for enrollment.

Advanced Placement (AP): Exams offered at the high school level only. University credits may be acquired through the AP examinations. These credits may be used to fill General Education requirements and may also be accepted as equivalent to specific courses.

Affidavit of Educational Purpose: A document signed by a student who is awarded one or more forms of federal financial aid.

Alumni: Graduates or former students of the institution.

Articulation: A term that is used to indicate that a course taken at another institution is equivalent to a course at the institution in which a student is planning to transfer.

Articulation Agreements: Documents that formally acknowledge how credits or degrees from other institutions equate to courses and requirements.

Assistant Resident Director: A live-in paraprofessional who assists in managing a residence hall. Assistant Resident Directors are usually full-time graduate students.

Associate Degree: A degree granted by a college or university after the satisfactory completion of the equivalent of a two-year, full-time program of study.

Audit: Registration in a course without credit or grade. Class attendance is required.

Award Letter: A letter from a college's financial aid office explaining the financial aid package that the school is offering a student. It outlines the amount and types of aid that will be awarded. The student must either accept or reject all or part of the award.

Bachelor's Degree: A degree in an academic discipline which typically requires completion of a minimum of 120 semester credit hours.

Board: A term used for the meal plan (as in, room and board) at the university.

Bulletin: A publication that lists the schedule of courses for an upcoming academic term. At some institutions, bulletins are considered the school's catalogue.

Bursar: An official in charge of funds, as at a college or university. Normally, this is the office you go to in order to pay your bills.

Call Number: A code that identifies a specific course.

Career Services: An office that is dedicated to assisting students with resume writing, interviewing skills, and job placement. Typically, career service offices offer assessment to help students discover their strengths and weaknesses with regard to choosing a major or finding a career.

Cashier: The financial officer of the university who receives payment of tuition and miscellaneous fees.

Certificate: A document certifying that one has fulfilled the requirements of and may practice in a certain vocation.

Class Rank: Student's ranking of being a freshman (less than 30 credits), sophomore (30-59 credits), junior (60-89 credits), or senior (90 or more credits), based on the number of college-level credit hours earned.

Closed Class: A class that has been filled by the maximum number of students allowed for that class.

Cognate: A course, or courses, related in some way to courses in a major. Cognates may be, and often are, courses outside the department of the degree program.

College: An academic division in a university. A college is composed of academic departments and is headed by a dean. For example, the College of Arts and Sciences or the College of Natural Sciences.

College Catalogue: Lists every department and course available at the institution.

College Level Examination Program (CLEP): A standardized examination in college-level subject matter. Subject examinations cover material offered in specific advanced-level courses. Credits may be acquired through the CLEP examinations. If a student passes the CLEP examination for a specific subject, they will receive college credit.

College Work Study: A form of financial aid based on need that provides students with paid employment while in school.

Cooperative Education: A program that provides for alternative class attendance and employment in business, industry, or government. Students typically are paid for their work.

Cooperative Housing: College-owned, operated, or affiliated housing in which students share room and board expenses and participate in household chores to reduce living expenses.

Commencement: A term used to refer to the graduation ceremony held in the last month of the school's spring, winter or summer semester.

Commercial Loan: A loan made through a bank or other lending institution for educational purposes as well as for a house, a car, or other consumer purchases.

Common Application: A college admission application that students may use to apply to any of 321 member colleges and universities in the United States. A Common Application reduces the workload of students who would otherwise have to complete separate applications to several colleges.

Commuter Student: One who lives at home and travels to the college.

Competency Test: A test that is used to determine if a student has the acquired knowledge of a college-level course. These tests are also referred to as placement test.

Complete Withdrawal: The process of withdrawing from all courses before a semester has ended. Students usually explore this option when they have a circumstance that does not allow them to continue.

Composite Major: When elements of two major programs are combined into one major program. For example, the Elementary Education/Special Education major is an approved composite of two different majors.

Concentration: A concentration (or option or emphasis) is a group of courses that are more similar to one another than to others in the degree program. For example, a student can major in History but their concentration is Early World History.

Concurrent Enrollment: When a high school student is enrolled in a university course for which the student simultaneously receives high school and university credit.

Continuing Education: Courses that students can take without pursuing a degree.

Continuing Education Unit (CEU): Recognition for participation in a non-credit program or workshop at a college or university.

Convocation: An opening ceremony to welcome new students. At some institutions, it is a lecture series that happens either at the beginning and/or during the academic year. At some institutions, convocations are mandatory.

Co-op: Two or more related internship work experiences.

Course Fee: A fee that is attached to a specific course, in addition to tuition.

Course Load: The number of credit hours carried by a student during a given semester. Generally, students need to average a minimum of 12 credit hours per semester in order to be considered full time.

Course Reference Number (CRN): A five-digit number used to select a specific course, lab, and/or recitation.

Corequisite: A course that must be taken at the same time as another course.

Credit Hour: A unit of academic credit measured in semester hours or quarter hours. One credit hour usually represents one hour of class time per week.

Credit Load: The total number of credits for which a student registers during a semester or session.

Cross-listed Course: A cross-listed course is interdisciplinary in nature and, therefore, is listed as a course offered under two or more departments.

Cumulative Index: A number that represents the average of all earned grades.

Curriculum: A series of courses that meet a particular academic or vocational goal.

Deadline: The date by which certain information must be received by any given office or unit.

Dean: A college or university administrative official. An academic dean usually heads a college within the university. However, some deans meet with students regarding disciplinary issues.

Declaration of Major: At some institutions, a process whereby students formally notify the Registrar's Office of the major that they choose to include in their degree program.

Deferred Admission: When a student is accepted for a specific term but chooses to defer his or her admission until a future term.

Degree: A title bestowed as official recognition for the completion of a curriculum. The bachelor's degree is the first-level degree granted normally upon completion of a four-year course of study in a given field. The master's degree is an advanced degree that requires at least one additional year beyond the bachelor's degree. The doctor's degree, or doctorate, is an advanced degree requiring at least three years beyond the bachelor's degree. The professional degrees of Juris Doctor (a law degree) and Doctor of Medicine require three and four years, respectively, beyond the pre-professional curricula. The honorary degree is bestowed in recognition of outstanding merit or achievement without reference to the fulfillment of academic course requirements.

Degree Audit: A summary of academic progress showing courses completed and courses needed. An official degree audit is normally done for graduating students once they have completed their application for graduation.

Degree Student: A student who has been admitted to a degree category and is seeking a bachelor's, master's, or doctoral degree in a planned course of study.

Department: A division of a college that offers instruction in a particular branch of knowledge, for example the Department of English.

Department Head: The administrative head of an academic department, sometimes referred to as department chair.

Dependent Student: A student who lives with and is at least partially supported by parents or a guardian and who is claimed by them as a dependent for income tax purposes or one to whom these conditions applied in the academic year prior to applying for financial aid.

Diploma Mill: A term used to describe an organization that awards academic degrees and diplomas usually without recognition by legitimate and official accrediting bodies.

Discipline: A subject area. For example, English, Spanish, religious studies, and elementary education.

Disenrollment: The process by which a student is dropped from all their courses due to non-payment of tuition or other university related action (e.g. suspension).

Dissertation: A written thesis by a candidate for a doctoral degree.

Doctorate: An academic degree of the highest level. It is usually earned after you have completed a master's degree, although you can begin working on it after having a bachelor's degree. The time to complete this degree depends upon if you are full-time or part-time. If you are full-time, it normally takes 7-8 years to complete. Although the Ph.D. (**Doctor of Philosophy**) is the most commonly known doctorate degree, there are well over twenty types. When a person earns a doctorate degree, he/she then are referred to with their title (e.g., Dr. James Taylor or James Taylor, Ph.D.) Professionals who hold a Ph.D. are not the same as M.Ds (medical doctors).

Drop/Add: The process used if students need to change a schedule for which they have already registered. This process usually can only occur during the first or second week of the semester.

Dual Major: Any two majors that are completed at the same time. Also referred to as double major.

Elective: A course that the student may study by choice but which may or may not be required for the student's particular degree.

Expected Family Contribution (EFC): An amount, determined by a formula that is specified by law, that indicates how much of a family's financial resources should be available to help pay for school. Factors such as taxable and non-taxable income, assets (such as savings and checking accounts), and benefits (for example, unemployment or Social Security) are all considered in this calculation. The EFC is used in determining eligibility for federal needs-based aid.

Faculty: Academic staff of a university: professors, lectures, and/or researchers.

Family Educational Rights and Privacy Act (FERPA): A law that (1) provides that students will have access to inspect or review their educational records and (2) protects the rights of a student to privacy by limiting access to the educational record without express written consent. These rights transfer to the student when he or she reaches the age of 18 or attends a school beyond the high school level.

Federal Family Education Loan Program (FFELP): Education loans provided by private lenders and guaranteed by the federal government. Subsidized and unsubsidized Federal Stafford Loans and parent PLUS loans are included in this program.

Fees: Charges that cover costs not associated with tuition. In many cases, fees cover costs associated with student activities (clubs, student organizations, athletics, and special events).

Financial Aid Money: Scholarships, grants, loans, and work study that is awarded to students to help reduce the cost of college.

Financial Aid Package: The total amount of financial aid a student receives. For example, grants, loans, or work-study are combined in a "package" to help meet the student's needs.

Financial Assistance Award: The total package consisting of a combination of scholarships, loans, and part-time employment.

Financial Assistance Counselor: A staff person who works in the financial aid office who reviews a student's application, awards financial assistance, and helps the student and parents in all aspects of financing their education.

Financial Aid Transcript (FAT): Designed for use by upper class students transferring to a new institution, a document required from each school previously attended whether financial assistance was received or not. This document is required by the school at which a student is applying for financial assistance.

Financial Need: The difference between the cost of attendance and the estimated family contribution. This amount is the total eligibility for financial assistance from all sources, and it is used in determining the total amount of a financial assistance award.

First Generation College Student (FGCS): College students whose parents have had no previous postsecondary experience.

First Time in College (FTIC): A first-year student entering with less then 12 hours of college credit.

Forbearance: A postponement of loan payments, granted by a lender or creditor, for a temporary period. This is granted to give the borrower time to make up for overdue payments.

Fraternity: A male student society formed for either academic and/or social purposes, into which members are initiated by invitation and/or by voluntarily, sign up themselves. The goal of most fraternities is to promote goodwill among its members and a social network among its members. Fraternities are usually named by two or three Greek letters. Fraternities are also known as Greek-letter societies.

Free Application for Federal Student Aid (FAFSA): The federal financial assistance application. This must be completed by all students who wish to be considered for financial assistance.

Full-Time Student: Normally a student registered for 12 or more credit hours during a semester.

General Education Requirements: A set of requirements that all candidates for a college degree, regardless of major, must satisfy.

Grace Period: The six-month period between the time you leave school and the time you must start paying back your loan.

Grade Point Average (GPA): Total number of grade points received for each grade divided by total number of credits attempted.

Graduate Student: A student who has earned a bachelor's degree and is enrolled for advanced work in a graduate school.

Graduation Audit: A formal, required evaluation of the student's academic record and program of study to determine the student's eligibility for graduation. The audit, initiated by a student's application for graduation, determines whether all university, degree, and program requirements have been met satisfactorily.

Grant: A type of financial assistance award that does not need to be repaid by the student.

Greek Letter Societies: Organizations that include academic honor societies, and fraternities or sororities.

Gross Income: The total income of a family, including salaries, wages, interest, social security benefits, and any other taxable and nontaxable income.

Helicopter Parent (slang): A parent who is very attentive to his or her child or children, when they start in college or university. Helicopter parents have the tendency to hover and not allow their child to make independent decisions. This term has been popularized by university officials in the last couple of years, due to the rise of more millennial age students starting postsecondary institutions.

Hold: An official action taken by the institution possibly to prevent student registration or receipt of grades and transcripts until a student satisfies a requirement. For example, a registration hold is placed on a student until he or she has met his or her financial obligations.

Honors Program: A program for high-achieving students within an institution.

Incomplete Grade (*I*): A temporary grade that may be assigned when a student is unable to complete all of the work in a course due to extenuating circumstances but not due to poor performance.

Independent Student: A student who is not financially dependent on any other person, expect a spouse, for support.

Independent Study: Credits earned by working on an independent research or reading project supervised by a faculty member.

In-State Student: A student who is a legal resident of the state in which he/she attends school.

Institutional Student Information Report (ISIR): The Institutional Student Information Report (ISIR) is the name for the electronic version of Student Aid Reports (SARs) delivered to schools by the FAFSA processors.

Interdisciplinary: Designating a combination of subject matter from two or more disciplines within a course or program.

Internship: An opportunity for students to combine a career-related work experience with academic coursework. In an internship, a student can gain supervised practical experience in a professional field. Internships may or may not count for academic credit, it is based on previous arrangements.

Lab: A class whereby students perform experiments in a laboratory. Labs are usually required for natural science courses such as Biology, Chemistry, Physics, etc. They are frequently offered concurrently with lecture courses in the same subject.

Lecture: When an instructor speaks to the class for the entire class period with little or no class interaction.

Living Learning Communities (LLC): Communities that are established to provide special settings where academic successes are combined with residential experiences. Living-Learning Communities are normally housed on a floor in a residence hall and focus on a theme, major, or other special interest. They usually support the interest of community members in conjunction with special academic or social programming.

Loan: Loaned money that must be repaid over a period. Typically, a student must repay the loan amount plus interest.

Major: An academic subject chosen as a field of specialization, requiring a specific course of study.

Matriculation: The process of applying and gaining acceptance into a degree program at a college or university.

Mentor: An individual that is more experienced, who guides and helps another individual.

Merit-Based Financial Aid: This kind of financial aid is given to students who meet requirements not related to financial needs. Most merit-based aid is awarded based on academic performance or potential and is given in the form of scholarships or grants.

Minor: The field of second emphasis. Fewer semester hours' credit is required for a minor than for a major.

Need-based Financial Aid: Financial aid given to students who are determined to be in financial need of assistance based on their income and assets and their families' income and assets.

Needs Analysis: A process of reviewing a student's financial assistance application to determine the amount of financial assistance for which a student is eligible. Completing a needs analysis form is the required first step in applying for most types of financial assistance.

Noncustodial Parent's Statement: When parents of an applicant are separated or divorced, financial information from both parents is requested. The Noncustodial Parent's Statement is a form for the noncustodial parent to use to report this information.

Non-Degree Seeking: A student enrolled in courses for credit that is not recognized by the institution as seeking a degree or formal award.

Non-Resident Alien: A person who is not a citizen or national of the United States and who is in this country on a visa or temporary basis and does not have the right to remain indefinitely.

Nontraditional Student: A college student who is older than the typical undergraduate college student (usually aged 17-23). Normally, nontraditional college students are students who return to school after years of being away or older adults who attend college in the evening or on a part-time basis.

Orientation: A program that is designed to enable new students to have a smooth transition into the institution. Although not all orientations are the same, at most orientations, students have the opportunity to learn about academic and social expectations, meet other students, learn about the institution's services and resources, get acquainted with the campus, and meet with campus administrators.

Outside Scholarships: Scholarships from organizations outside the university such as corporations, foundations, service clubs, and local organizations. Often these scholarships are awarded directly to the student.

Overload: A process in which a student may obtain permission from their advisor to register for an increased credit load (typically 18 or more credits).

Part-time: The status of a student registered for fewer than usually twelve credits during a regular semester or quarter.

Pass/Fail: An option given in some classes whereby students may choose to take a course on a pass/fail basis. A letter grade is not given; the student either passes or fails.

Pell Grant: A federal student aid program for undergraduates. For undergraduate students, first baccalaureate degree only. The amount of the award ranges from $400 to $4,050, subject to Congressional appropriations, and is reduced for students who enroll part-time. It is only given to students who demonstrate financial need.

Perkins Loan: A low fixed interest federal loan for both undergraduate and graduate students with exceptional financial need.

Personal Statement: Essays used by admissions committees to learn more about their applicants. Personal statements are also known as the application essay. Personal statements are usually required by schools that are competitive. They are very common for graduate and professional school admission.

PIN Number: A personal identification number that is used as a password. The pin number is usually required in order to register online.

Placement Test: A test given to determine the appropriate level at which to place a student in certain courses. Placement tests are usually required before you can enroll in a class.

PLUS Loan: Loans that enable parents with good credit histories to borrow the education expenses of each child who is a dependent undergraduate student enrolled at least part-time.

Portfolio: An arrangement of projects, documents and/or artwork that is used in some majors and degree programs for admission decisions, assessment, career placement, or graduation requirements.

Postsecondary Institution: Any proprietary or vocational school, college, or university that offers education and training to students beyond the high school level. It is also referred to as higher education.

Practicum: A course of study designed especially for the preparation of teachers and clinicians. A practicum involves the supervised practical application of previously studied classes and theory.

Prerequisite: A course that must be completed prior to taking another course.

Priority Registration: The order in which students may register for classes. A priority registration schedule indicates the earliest possible day a student may register for classes.

Professor: A college teacher of the highest rank. At a college or university, there are assistant, associate, visiting, and full professors.

Probation (Academic): An academic status indicating that a student's cumulative index is below 2.0 GPA.

Promissory Note: A contract stating the terms of agreement of a promise by one party to pay a sum of money to the other. The promissory note usually has to be signed before you can take out a student loan.

Quarter System: The division of the academic year into four equal parts.

Reading Day: Usually the day before and/or the week of final exams when no exams or classes are scheduled.

Recitation: A class period especially in association with and for review of a lecture.

Registrar: The administrative officer who maintains enrollment records and certifies the academic standing, as well as the fulfillment of graduation requirements, for all enrolled students.

Registration: The act of enrolling in classes.

Remedial Course: A course that will not satisfy degree requirements, are not transferable, and are not calculated in a student's grade point average. They usually serve as a prerequisite class for credited classes.

Residence Hall: A building that houses both formal and informal living learning communities. Although many people refer to residence halls as dorms, the environment of the building is not just were students sleep. It is the place where the majority of learning outside of the classroom takes place.

Residency: A classification for tuition purposes. In-state residents pay lower tuition than nonresidents.

Resident Assistant: The Resident Assistant (RA) is a full-time student who is employed by the university or college to live on campus and assigned to a particular floor or area in the Residence Halls. The RA assists residents in meeting their educational, interpersonal, and social needs relative to their living environment. They also assist with crisis intervention and provide educational and social activities for residents. Also referred to as resident advisor, community assistant, fellow, etc.

Resident Director: A live-in educator who manages a residence hall. Resident Directors are full-time professionals who usually supervise Resident Assistants. They are also involved in advising students, crisis intervention, completing administrative tasks (room transfers, maintenance issues, keys), setting limits on the floor and throughout the building, and implementing floor and building events (programs). Additionally, at most institutions, Resident Directors meet with students who violate hall and/or university policies (noise, alcohol, drug, etc.). Some schools also refer to Resident Directors as Hall Directors, Area Coordinators, etc.

Resume: A document containing a summary or listing of previous or relevant job experience and education, usually for the purpose of obtaining an interview when seeking employment. Students should try to have a resume done no later then the end of their freshman year.

Reserve Officers Training Corps (ROTC): A scholarship program offered by many colleges and universities wherein the military covers the cost of tuition, fees, and textbooks and also provides a monthly allowance. In exchange, scholarship recipients participate in summer training while in college and fulfill a service commitment after college.

Rolling Admissions: A policy where admissions offices review and decide on applications as they are received until there are no openings left in the entering class. When a school has a rolling admissions policy, they usually do not have a deadline for applications; however, it is on a first come, first serve basis.

Rush: A drive by a Greek letter society on a college campus to recruit new members. Depending upon the college or university, rushes usually take place during the beginning of the school year.

SAT: A standardized test used for college admission in the United States. The SAT consists of three major sections: Mathematics, Critical Reading, and Writing. Each section receives a score on the scale of 200–800.

Security Deposit: Money paid upfront in order to protect the provider of a product or service against damage or nonpayment by the buyer. For example, landlords usually require a security deposit of one month's rent when a tenant signs a lease to cover the possibility that the tenant will move out without paying the last month's rent or that the tenant will inflict substantial damage on the property while living there. Before you can move into campus housing you must submit a security deposit with your application.

Service Learning: A fairly new experiential learning experience that balances the needs of student and community members. Additionally, service learning connects service and learning through a reflective process. Students tend to gain a sense of social responsibility, increased intellectual development, and career development.

Scholarship: Student financial aid based on academic achievement, need, or a combination of factors. Scholarships do not have to be repaid.

Semester: A 14 or 15 week period of study. There are two semesters in an academic year.

Sorority: A female student society formed for either academic and/or social purposes, into which members are initiated by invitation, or they voluntarily sign up themselves. The goal of most sororities is to promote sisterhood and a social network among its members. Sororities are usually named by two or three Greek letters. Sororities are also considered Greek-letter societies.

Specialization: An approved area of study, having a specific curriculum within a particular graduate degree.

Stafford Loans: Stafford loans are student loans. They are provided by banks and are federally regulated.

Student Activities: An office or department at a college or university that provides opportunities for students to be involved in the life of the school. The office usually oversees all organizations to which students are members.

Student Aid Report (SAR): A form sent to the student after submitting the FAFSA to the federal processor. The SAR shows the information processed and indicates Pell Grant eligibility.

Student ID Number: A multi-code that uniquely identifies each student. At some institutions, the social security number is used as the student ID number.

Study Abroad Program: A program that gives students the opportunity to pursue educational opportunities in another country. Normally, students are enrolled in classes while studying abroad, and credits are transferred back to their home institution. Students can typically find out about these programs in the International Education office, Study Abroad or Foreign Language Department.

Subsidized Loan: A loan awarded based on financial need. When students take out subsidized loans they are not charged any interest before they begin repayment or during deferment periods.

Syllabus: The document that a professor provides as a course outline. A syllabus will usually include assignments, due dates, test dates, grading procedures, and attendance policies and an overview of the course. It is usually provided on the first day of class.

Taxable Income: Income included on tax returns: salaries, wages, tips, interest, and dividends minus deductions and exemptions.

Teaching Assistant (TA): A graduate or undergraduate student with teaching responsibilities.

Traditional Student: Students who are the typical undergraduate college student, usually aged 17-23.

Transcript: An official copy of a student's academic record available through either the Records and Registration Office or Registrar's Office.

Transfer Credit: Credit that was earned at another college or university.

Tuition: The amount charged per semester credit hour for instruction at a college or university.

Verification: A process of review to determine the accuracy of the information on a student's financial assistance application.

Undeclared Major: The status for students who have not yet decided upon a major program. First-year students usually come in as undeclared majors.

Undergraduate: A college or university student who has not yet earned a bachelor's degree.

Unit: A specific measure of value ascribed to satisfactory completion a course of study. Sometimes referred to as credits or hours.

University: An assembly of colleges, each specializing in a different field.

Unsubsidized Loan: A loan that is not granted based on need. Unsubsidized loans charge interest from the time the loan is awarded until the time it is paid in full. These loans have no grace period.

Withdraw: The process of voluntarily leaving a course or the university without academic penalty. A "W" letter grade will be placed on the student's transcript for each course attempted. Typically, once the class is repeated, the W letter grade will be replaced by the new letter grade.

Work-Study Programs: A program offered by many colleges and universities that allow students to work part time during the school year as part of their financial aid package. Students can usually apply for these jobs in the student employment office or financial aid office.

W-2: Statement used for income tax purposes. W-2 forms are sent to an employee and show gross earnings and deductions (such as federal, state, and local income taxes and FICA) for a calendar year. The W-2 Form is a necessary document for filing for financial aid as it can determine if a student is eligible for financial aid. It is also called a wage and tax statement.

Index

978-0-595-47509-4
0-595-47509-4

CPSIA information can be obtained at www.ICGtesting.com
Printed in the USA

267980BV00003B/136/P